The Ghost Wi

A haunting collection of stories about the evil in everyday things – superbly written tales which burrow into the imagination and stay there.

Also by Alison Prince

Goodbye Summer

The Ghost Within

ALISON PRINCE

MAMMOTH

First published in Great Britain 1984
by Methuen Children's Books Ltd
Magnet edition published 1986
Published 1989 by Mammoth
an imprint of Mandarin paperbacks
Michelin House, 81 Fulham Road, London SW3 6RB

Mandarin is an imprint of the Octopus Publishing Group

ISBN 0 7497 0222 2

A CIP catalogue record for this title
is available from the British Library

Printed in Great Britain
by Cox & Wyman Ltd, Reading

Contents

ONE

The Lilies

I stopped at the Chapel on my way home from school, to see if they had been throwing their flowers away again. It was an ugly building made of bricks as dark as ox liver, with an iron railing in front of it with spikes on top. My mother said it looked as if it was meant for cold storage rather than worship. The Chapel seemed black and awful to me, like the smell of gas or like the rubber galoshes Mrs Parfitt across the road wore over her shoes on wet days. But I had to see about the flowers.

I pushed the iron gate open and went round the side of the building. Its windows were high up and there were slabs of stone in the wall commemorating the death of people with names like Edwin Pugh and Gladys Bowker. A neat, sad little row of lobelia plants set among granite chips looked up at me mournfully but the salvias planted behind them didn't say a word. Salvias, though brave souls, are sadly lacking in imagination.

Outside the back door of the Chapel there was a dustbin. I took the lid off and looked in. Sure enough, on top of a pile of used cardboard beakers there were three dead lilies. Their long white blooms were brown and shrivelled now, and their stems were slimy from being too long in water. I lifted them carefully out of the bin.

The back door opened and the Reverend Evans came out. His face knotted in a frown when he saw me. 'Sarah Mulloy, you are at it again!' he said angrily. I dropped the lid back on the dustbin and fled. 'I'll be coming to see your mother!' he shouted after me. 'What you are doing is pagan, do you hear me? Pagan!'

I ran down the street with my hair flying out behind me and the dead lilies flopping up and down in my arms. The terraces of houses seemed to bump up and down with me as I ran, jogging behind their stone steps and clipped privet hedges as if they were alive instead of dozing with half-shut eyes behind their curtained windows. Welsh houses were never considered to be respectable unless their curtains were kept almost closed. On the down-hill side of the street the land fell away to the disused railway and the greened-over slag heaps, and on the other side the mountain reared up against the sky.

I hated the Reverend Evans. I hated the way his black jacket was too small for him, with the sleeves too short so that his wrists poked out and made his brown-mottled hands seem even bigger. I hated the dog-collar which cut into his thick neck, and the pale, square face and the grey hair sticking up in a crest like an angry parrot.

I turned up the hill between the Co-op and the Black Bull, where the doorsteps were high at one corner and low at the other because of the steep slope, then turned left past Mrs Parfitt's. Our house was the last in that narrow street. There was nothing after us except the mountain. I could see my mother in the garden – at least I could see the top half of her above the waist-high lupins and Canterbury bells. Her head was bent as she stooped to talk to the flowers, and strands of hair were escaping as always from the pinned-up mass of it. She looked up and saw me. 'There you are, my darling!' she called. She had never lost her Irish accent although it was years since she and my father had come across from Ireland in search of work. I had been born here and my father lay buried in the steep cemetery behind the Catholic church; but my mother had never become Welsh. She made her way between the flowers to see what I carried.

'Ah, the poor souls,' she said when she saw the lilies. She gathered them gently from me and set off round the side of the house to the back garden, sloping away up the hill. At the end was our graveyard. A spade leaned against the wall and I took it and began to dig a hole big enough to accommodate the lilies. When it was done, my mother knelt down and laid the dead flowers in it. 'From earth you came – to earth you shall return,' she said. 'And God's blessing be upon you.' I said, 'Amen,' then shovelled the earth back on top of the lilies. We wrote their name and the date on a small white marker and stuck it in the earth to show where they lay. Our graveyard was full of such markers, like a field of small plastic tombstones.

'What's for tea?' I asked, dusting my hands.

'I think we'll have scrambled eggs,' my mother said.

We had just finished when there was a banging at the front door.

'Will you listen to that?' said my mother, not moving. 'Who would it be, coming to the front? That door has never been opened in years.'

'I'll go and tell them to come round the back,' I said, getting up, but with a sinking of the heart, for something told me it would be the Reverend Evans. Sure enough, it was. His black coat was tightly buttoned and his large face was grim. He followed me round to the kitchen door but his eyes were darting about and instead of coming in he stopped and said: 'I want you to show me the place.'

'What place?' I asked, although I knew what people said about us. And I knew he listened.

'The place where you bury these flowers,' he said. 'There has been a lot of wild talk going on. People murmur of witchcraft. It's bad for the village.'

My mother had come to the kitchen door in time to hear this. 'The village!' she said with contempt. 'All scrubbed white doorsteps and drawn curtains but devil a one of them has a good word to say about another. They're a black-hearted, treacherous lot. Don't be talking to me about the village.'

The flowers were listening and they shrank together a little. There was a bad feeling from the man with his angry hair and his pale, bulging eyes.

'We only lay the flowers to rest,' I told him. 'So that their bodies return to the soil and their souls return to God, from whence they came.'

'Sacrilege!' shouted the Reverend Evans, raising a quivering fist against the sky. 'I will not have pagan rites conducted in this village! Where is the place? I will find it!' He charged up the sloping garden like a black bull and stopped as if pole-axed when he came to the graveyard.

'Disgusting!' he said between clenched teeth, and beads of sweat stood out on his forehead. 'A parody of human decency!'

He grabbed the spade which stood against the wall and started to swipe wildly at the little plastic gravestones, scattering them aside and cutting gouges in the earth. A thin cry went up from the foxgloves and the shaggy red poppies and was echoed along the grey leaves of the alyssum and through the wild thyme which grew between the flagstones, until the whole garden vibrated in protest.

My mother wasted no words. She reached out a brown hand and grabbed the spade, and for a few seconds she and the Reverend Evans were locked in a tussle for its possession. But my mother was used to hard work and she was stronger than the flabby man for whom a smile was a taxing of the muscles. She wrested the spade away from him and its sudden loss threw him off his balance. He grabbed for support at a great sunflower whose face was turned to the sky as if trying not to look at the man, but its thick, hairy stem broke in his grasp. He fell awkwardly, flinging his hand up as if to grab at something else, and the back of his head smacked against the garden wall with a sound like the breaking of a huge boiled egg.

'Ohhhh,' breathed the flowers in a waft of scent and relief.

'The stupid man,' said my mother, staring down at the

Reverend Evans who lay like a sack of soot among the plastic gravestones. 'He should have stayed down there in his Chapel.'

It was very quiet. The broken-off sunflower lay across the black-clad chest, smiling blandly up at the sky. Its broad, dinner-plate face was studded with ripening seeds, so it had no resentment. I knelt down and looked carefully at the Reverend Evans. His face was very white and it didn't have any meaning. He seemed to have turned into a thing instead of a person. A trickle of blood was making its way over the back of his stiff dog-collar to soak into the earth. The plants would like that, I thought. As good as a dead rat in a leek trench.

My mother stood leaning on the spade, looking down at the black heap of a man. 'When I die,' she said thoughtfully, 'you must bury me here.'

'Not in the churchyard?' I asked. 'Not with my father?' But I knew what she meant.

'It would be such a pity to waste me,' she said, and ran her finger gently up the wide-open bells of the campanula which leaned against her apron.

It took us a long time to bury the Reverend Evans. Not only was he very large, but redisposing the mortal remains of the flowers already in the graveyard was time-consuming. At last it was all done and the earth was raked smooth between the neat rows of little plastic gravestones. The presence of the man had created quite a hump.

I sat back on my heels. It was nearly dark. 'Shouldn't we put a marker in for him?' I said.

My mother looked faintly puzzled. 'But he is fertiliser, child,' she said. So we put the tools away in the shed and went indoors for a mug of cocoa before bed.

I felt a little worried. The house plants did their best to console me, holding up the gentle patterning of their leaves and stretching their petals wide despite the lateness of the night, but I was fearful of what the morning would bring. I had good reason to fear the village people, for the children I went to school with had all been told by their parents that my mother was a witch. And I, the witch's child, was the one whose hands were burned with hot match-ends behind the cycle shed, to see if it hurt. I had no friends at school. Although each face was different, made individual by a freckled nose or a missing tooth, the eyes were all the same, lit with a cruel curiosity. Tomorrow was Saturday, a blessed respite from torment. I could stay with the flowers and they would heal the wounds of the week with the simple truth of their existence. But what of the Reverend Evans? People would come looking for him.

'Don't look so worried, my darling,' said my mother as I picked up my candle to go to bed. 'God is in the garden. It is vain of us to be troubled when He knows everything.' And I kissed her and went up the stairs with the candle-shadows leaping on either side of me, up to my little room where the morning-glory had wandered in through my window under the thatch and now waited with closed buds for the dawn.

The sun was streaming in when I woke. The morning glory had opened her china-blue flowers and I ran to the window and looked out. My mother was at the end of the garden beside the graveyard, on her knees. Her hands were clasped and her head bent in prayer. That was strange, I thought. She would hardly pray for the soul of the Reverend Evans. One did not pray for fertiliser. I put on my dress and ran downstairs.

As I approached the graveyard I saw why my mother was kneeling. The earth which we had left raked and bare the night before was green with young plants. Poppies and sweet williams, snapdragons and pansies and love-in-a-mist were all thrusting their way upwards, growing from their dead parents before our very eyes. And chief among them all were the pale spears of the three white lilies which I had brought home only yesterday from the dustbin behind the Chapel. I could not believe what I saw. The God of our garden had truly wrought a miracle. I met my mother's eyes and found in her face the same astonishment and gratitude which I felt myself. And there was, too, the same effort to suppress an unspeakable giggle.

'The lilies,' I began carefully. 'We put them – ' I could not say it.

My mother composed her lips to banish any hint of a smile before she completed my sentence. 'Underneath the Reverend Evans,' she said with precision. 'Yes.' We stared in silence at the sharp tips of the lily shoots, already a handspan tall. Then my mother got to her feet, dusted the earth from her long skirt and came back to the kitchen with me, for she had left a batch of bread dough proving before the fire.

They never found the Reverend Evans although ours was one of the first houses the police came to. They searched the cottage then went into the garden and stood there in their thick serge uniforms, staring about. The flowers stared back rather rudely, but the policemen did not notice. 'What would you be looking for?' my mother asked them, and the fat policeman whose chinstrap made pink grooves down the sides of his face said: 'Signs of recent digging.'

The flowers tittered among themselves. There was not an inch of soil to be seen between them, and the graveyard in particular was smothered with blooms of amazing size and opulence. The policeman's unhappy gaze rested on the three tall spikes of white lilies which stood like cathedral spires among the shorter plants. There was a brooding inwardness about them which would arrest the attention of anyone with the wit to see it. The policeman nodded at them grudgingly. 'Nice, those, he said. 'Sort of – pure.' And then he and his mate trudged across the road to Mrs Parfitt's.

Time went by and at last I was able to leave school. I sold vegetables from a little stall at our gate, for the plants were glad to see their fruit put to its natural use as food for other living beings. But the barbarians who asked me to cut my flowers for them were turned away with no words wasted. Dry grasses and the beautiful skeletons of Honesty they were welcome to, but nobody could make me slice through the stem of one of my living friends.

One warm evening I found my mother lying in the garden among the flowers, quiet and still, while the snow-in-summer touched her lips and her eyes with its silver fingers. I wept for the loss of her and the flowers respected my grief. But they told me that time is unimportant and that death is only part of the pattern of growing and consuming and rebirth, and after a while their wisdom made me calm. I knew what I had to do. 'It would be a pity to waste me,' she had said.

I suppose I should have waited until dark. The villagers who came for a pound of tomatoes and a cucumber stared when they saw me digging so deeply in the new graveyard we had made where the end of the path used to be, and they did not seem to like the sight of my mother lying there among the flowers. A little while later the policemen came, and brought with them some men wearing long white coats. I was very angry with them because they started to interfere with what I was doing, and it was no business of theirs. They dragged me away from my half-dug grave and stabbed me in the arm with something sharp. I was not in the least tired, for the sun still shone in the sky and it was nowhere near bedtime, but sleep came swimming over me. I cried out and the white lilies remembered how I had saved them from their death behind the Chapel, and leaned towards me anxiously. I clutched at their smooth stems but I fell down, down, past the rosettes of the hollyhocks and past their strong leaves and even past the startled little rock rose, down to a darkness like that of the earth itself.

I woke in this strange place where the sky is hard and white, and terribly near. All my flowers had come with me and the white walls were alive with them, touching me gently with leaf and tendril. After a while the people in white coats came in and stood round my bed, talking. They moved through strong stems and fleshy green leaves as if the room was empty, and the flowers laughed to see it.

My hands were aching and when I looked to see why this was, I found that I was gripping the stems of the three white lilies with all my strength. The people noticed this and tried to uncurl my fingers so that they could take my lilies away, but I screamed and held on tightly and at last the people went away.

When I was alone again the flowers wept. I stared at the hard white man-made sky which was so near above my head and knew that beyond it was the sun. I felt the strength of the lilies in my hands and the host of flowers crowded round me, dew-wet with their tears. Yes, they said. Yes. The strength of the lilies can penetrate all obstacles. Remember the Reverend Evans.

I got up from the bed where I had woken, and laid the lilies carefully on the white sheet. Their dying faces smiled up. Trust us, they said. We will free you from this place. Carefully, I climbed back onto the bed, and carefully lay down with the lilies underneath me, their heads below my heart.

A gale of fragrance comes from my flowers, for soon we will be out in the real world again, in God's blue, endless sky. Already the skin in the middle of my back is pricked by the spear-sharp tips of the growing lilies.

TWO

Herb

'What with mice and blasted Communism,' said Pip's mother as she opened a tin of beans crossly, 'you might as well not have a father at all. I don't know how he finds time for the milk round.' The cigarette in her mouth had burned down until its glowing end almost touched her lips. Squinting horribly, she detached it and ground the butt into the wet potato peelings in the sink-tidy.

Pip stared out at the shed across the yard where Geoff Bickerstaff's large silhouette could be seen moving behind the window. 'I don't mind the Communism,' he said. 'At least he's out with his leaflets. What I hate is the way he kills the baby mice when there's too many.'

Pip's older sister Meryl, sprawled on the sofa with her make-up things spread round her, looked up from her mirror and said, 'He's got to, stupid. He only wants the really good ones that might win a prize at a show. We'd be over-run with the beastly things else. Bad enough as it is.'

'Bad enough with people,' said Edna Bickerstaff darkly. She dumped the beans in a saucepan and slapped it on the flaring gas.

Meryl applied some puce eye-shadow and said, 'Blooming well wish there weren't so many of *us*. I'd have a room to myself if it wasn't for Janice. And look at the rows between you and Kevin, Pip. Fancy having to draw a chalk line down the middle of the floor!'

'It was his idea!' protested Pip. 'The way he goes on, you'd think he was *giving* me half *his* room.'

'Well, he was here first,' said Meryl. 'We all were. You're

the afterthought. If anyone ought to have got the chop, it's you.'

'Not his fault,' said Edna in half-hearted defence of her youngest. She cut two slices of bread and rammed them into the toaster. 'I'm not waiting supper for Kevin, nor Janice neither. Don't know what they think they're doing, but I'm going to Bingo, so if they're late in they'll have to get their own. Pip, go and tell your dad to wash his hands if he's finished dishing out the mice their beastly muesli. Blasted mice,' she added, poking at the beans with a spoon. The saucepan, unstirred since it was put on the intense heat, was beginning to give off a smell of burning. Pip wrinkled his nose in distaste as he went out of the back door.

The sky was a pale yellow colour, hazy and glowing in the September evening. A faint whiff of watery, weedy canal-scent freshened the dusty air, contrasting sharply with the kitchen and the beans. Pip had always wished he could see the canal from the house, but even from his bedroom window it was hidden by the roof of the furniture warehouse whose wall formed the end of the Bickerstaffs' yard. Pip dreamed about the sea sometimes, miles and miles of sparkling water that stretched to the horizon. But when he approached it the water always shrank away from him as if someone had pulled the plug out of the ocean bed, and all that was left was mud and broken bottles.

Pip stood in the yard among the cast-off bits of Kevin's various motor bikes, sniffing the canal smell. That was the good thing about Uncle Herb's house, he thought. The canal ran right past the bottom of the garden – if you could call all those weeds a garden. Pip smiled. He didn't mind it like that. Perhaps he would go round there after supper. His mother banged on the window. 'Hurry up!' she shouted. Pip's day-dreaming infuriated her.

Reluctantly, Pip knocked on the door of the shed with his knuckles and called: 'Supper's ready! His father opened the door. A very small black and white mouse dangled by its tail from the thumb and finger of one hand. In the other he held a pencil. Geoff Bickerstaff's face was so thickly covered with hair that he appeared to have virtually no features except for a sharply pointed nose in the middle of it all. The rest was hidden under the wiry ginger beard and the shaggy hair, and his eyes were masked behind very thick wire-framed spectacles with circular lenses. What was good enough for Karl Marx, Geoff would say proudly when people laughed at these spectacles, was good enough for him. For a long time Pip had been convinced that his father had somehow inherited Karl Marx's own glasses. Uncle Herb had laughed when he heard of this belief. 'Old Geoff?' he said. 'Not on your life. He took a copy of *Das Kapital* down to the optician and showed him the picture of Marx on the front. Cost him a mint of money to get glasses made exactly the same.' Somehow Pip had felt less afraid of his father after that.

'Tell her I'm coming,' said Geoff. Pip glanced briefly at the stacked cages, each one identical and scrupulously clean, and the bench with its neat row of food bins and its weighing scale. He knew what the pencil in his father's hand was for. You put the mouse on a flat surface, held the pencil firmly across the back of its neck and picked the mouse up by its tail, thus breaking its neck. Pip had seen it done. As Geoff moved to the bench with the black and white mouse, he turned away and shut the door behind him.

An hour later Pip was banging on another door with his knuckles. The faded blue paint was peeling off and a tall hollyhock leaned across it like a drunken man. From inside came the sound of a trumpet being played lazily, the slow blues moving with a tired, loose-jointed gait like someone who has worked hard all day and is whistling on the way home. And yet there was more to it than that. Pip fingered the drying seed pods on the hollyhock's stem and stared across the waist-high tangle of weeds to where the canal ran sluggishly beyond the broken fence. A narrow, trodden path led through the weeds to the water's edge and Pip remembered coming here on hot summer days to find his uncle standing on the bank, propped like a scarecrow on his two sticks, staring down at the water as if, like Pip, he dreamed of the sea.

Pip's spine tingled with the odd feeling which Uncle Herb's trumpet always aroused in him, and his mouth twitched with a smile which was near to tears. He waited patiently by the door, not repeating his knock. He knew Herb would have heard him the first time. He would answer when he was ready. The slow notes were almost despairing and yet they implied that nothing mattered much. Nobody expected life to be good, but you could still enjoy it. In a way.

A flock of starlings flew across the yellow sky towards the city where they would roost on the ledges of the buildings. Even above Herb's trumpet, Pip heard the whirr of their wings. The tune ended.

'Come in!' shouted Herb.

Pip went in. His uncle was sitting on a wooden chair beside the table where half a loaf, some cheese and a pot of pickled onions still stood on the checked cloth. His trumpet lay across his knees.

'Hello, Buddy Bolden,' said Herb.

'Hello,' said Pip. He slid himself onto the chair on the opposite side of the table with a small, happy sigh. A piece of bindweed had grown through a crack in the wall and dangled aimlessly into the room. Herb got a tin of tobacco and a packet of papers out of his pocket and slowly made himself a cigarette. He lit it and exhaled a cloud of smoke. He was as broad-shouldered as his brother Geoff, his face similarly bearded, but there the resemblance ended. Herb was dark, his beard grizzled with grey, and his eyes were a clear blue made more intense by the black eyelashes which surrounded them. Meryl said she thought he used mascara, but Pip knew Herb would greet such an idea with his tired smile. 'Daft piece,' he would say.

'Cup of tea?' offered Herb.

'Yes, please,' said Pip. He got to his feet. The kettle steamed gently on the Aga. Pip felt the teapot which stood on the table and said, 'Shall I make some fresh?'

'Why not?' said Herb. 'Live dangerously.'

Pip watched his uncle out of the corner of his eye as he made the tea. Herb was sitting very still this evening, his head angled back a little in an attitude of uncomplaining endurance. His two walking sticks were hooked over the arm of his chair. 'How are your legs?' asked Pip.

'Not so bad,' said Herb as he always did. Pip glanced at the thick black surgical boots which stuck out from the bottom of Herb's jeans, and stirred the tea slowly. There was silence as he put the pot on the table and found himself a mug. Then Herb said: 'How's your life?'

Pip shrugged. He thought of the black and white mouse in his father's hand, of the smell of burning beans. Of Meryl saying, 'If anyone ought to have got the chop, it's you.' He pursed his lips as if to whistle a snatch of the tune Herb had been playing and suddenly there was a hot tightness in his throat and he could not whistle or talk. He ducked his head, doubling his hands into fists.

'Don't let the buggers get you down,' said Herb. Then he added, 'Geoff still handing out leaflets at the factory gates, is he?'

After a few moments Pip managed to smile. 'He got arrested last week,' he said. 'For trying to stick a poster on the mayoral car. "Equality Not Privilege", it said. They let him go, though. Kevin says they think he's a nutter.'

'Geoff doesn't like mayors,' said Herb. He thought, then smiled faintly. 'I suppose he'd like us all in the same little units, like his mice.'

'I don't know,' said Pip. He poured out two mugs of tea then said: 'Couldn't I come and live here? I could look after you and go to school in the day. There's too many of us at home – they're always saying so.'

Herb shook his head. 'Nice idea, Buddy,' he said. 'But They wouldn't like it, you know.' He gestured vaguely at the unseen cohorts of authority outside. 'You're not supposed to look after anyone when you're eleven. Someone's supposed to look after *you*.'

'But I'm starting at the Comprehensive next week,' protested Pip. 'I'm nearly grown up.'

'Have a heart,' said Herb. 'What you trying to do, get me locked up?'

Pip's mind seethed with rebellion. 'I just can't bear the way things are,' he said. 'There must be something different.' He thought of his dream of the sea. 'Space,' he said, sweeping out an arm and endangering the teapot. 'Some way of really *being*.' The trumpet's music, the dream sea and the smell of the canal fused in his mind so that he felt as if he would blow up. His uncle looked at him. 'That's your immortal soul, Buddy,' he said. 'Old Geoff feels the same, you know, but with him it takes the form of trying to change the world. With me it's the blues.' He glanced down at his wasted legs. 'Couldn't have been much else,' he said in a matter-of-fact way. 'But I reckon it would have been the blues anyway.'

There was a pause. They sipped their tea and looked at each other consideringly. Herb could manage all right really, Pip supposed. He played with a jazz band quite often. They came to pick him up in the van when there was a gig on, and it wasn't as if Herb played a guitar or a synthesiser. He didn't have a pile of amplifiers and things to hump around.

Herb said suddenly: 'You ever wanted to play the trumpet?'

Pip blushed. He had always considered it to be a grown-up activity like driving a car.

'Well, have you?' Herb persisted.

'It'd be great,' said Pip. 'I mean, one day.'

'Whaddayer mean, one day?' demanded Herb with a flash of energy. 'You want to start when you're young. I'll teach you if you like.'

'Do you mean – you think I really could?' Pip looked at the trumpet lying across Herb's thin legs and was moved by a painful excitement.

'You won't sound like Louis Armstrong the minute you pick it up,' said Herb, 'but you can learn. Everyone's got to start, for Chrissake.' He handed the trumpet across the table to Pip, who took it awkwardly. In Herb's hands it looked so natural. So much part of him. He fingered the valves tentatively, then raised it to his lips and blew. Nothing happened.

'It's not like cooling your tea,' said Herb. 'You've got to put enough air in that thing to make it vibrate. Imagine there's a bit of tissue paper on the tip of your tongue and you're trying to spit it into the mouthpiece. Like, 'Tfff!' He demonstrated. 'Keep trying. You'll find it.'

Pip kept trying. He blew in every way he could think of until his eyes were watering and the top of his head felt as if it was coming off, but he produced nothing more than a series of unmusical squawks from the trumpet. He stared down at it while he recovered his breath. Please, he said to it silently, please play for me. He raised it to his lips again, gathered his breath steadily and blew. And it was right. The trumpet played a loud, quivering note.

Herb grinned at Pip's expression of surprise. 'That's it!' he said.

'It feels as if it's alive!' exclaimed Pip.

'Of course the bloody thing's alive,' said Herb. 'Come on, Buddy – play it again.'

In the weeks that followed Pip went almost every day to Herb's house. As the daylight shortened and the evenings grew dark earlier he spent long hours in the warm kitchen wrestling with the intricacies of playing the trumpet. Guided by Herb, he quickly came to understand how the instrument worked. At first he was embarrassed by his many mistakes and inadequacies, but Herb remained patient and light-hearted and soon Pip realised that his own feelings about himself did not matter. The important thing was to think about the playing. Herb made him buy some manuscript paper and showed him in sketchy pencil dots and lines that music had a written language. 'It's okay playing what's in your own head,' he explained, 'that's half of it – but you've got to be able to read what other people have written. That way you get into their heads as well.'

One evening Herb said: 'Clear the stuff off that old trunk in the corner, Buddy, and have a look in it. There might be some music you can use.' Lifting the trunk's lid, Pip found a stack of dog-eared music with pictures of beaming Negro faces printed sideways on the covers. He lifted it all out and dumped it on the table beside Herb. 'M'm,' said his uncle, thumbing through it, 'could be a bit complicated yet. You'll come to it, though.' Standing beside him, Pip read the titles. 'Twelfth Street Rag', 'Black Bottom Stomp', 'Buddy Bolden's Blues'. 'Hey!' he said, pointing, 'That's what you call me, Buddy Bolden!'

'That's right,' said Herb. And in a voice so rough with home-rolled cigarettes that it was hardly a voice at all, he sketched the tune. 'Thought I heard Buddy Bolden say, You're awful, you're terrible, Take it all away . . .' He stopped. 'Don't know why I fixed you with Buddy Bolden,' he said. 'Just sort of happened.'

'How does the rest of it go?' asked Pip.

Herb leaned his head back against his chair. 'Thought I heard Buddy Bolden shout,' he sang, 'Open up that window, let the bad air out. Open up that window, let the foul air out, I thought I heard him shout.' He reached out his hand and Pip wordlessly gave him the trumpet. The notes Herb blew were in the same key (magically, Pip thought) as his singing had been, but they took off with easy freedom and wove an idle, rhythmic fantasy arising from the theme. Although Pip was beginning to think in a more technical way about music, it still made the hair creep on his head to hear his uncle play. When Herb blew the last lingering note and put the trumpet down Pip sighed. 'I'll never play like you,' he said. 'You really are terrific.'

Herb gave his tired smile. 'Great to have a fan,' he said.

'You've got lots of fans,' protested Pip. 'I mean, you play with the band –'

'Used to,' said Herb.

Pip looked at him. 'What do you mean?' he asked.

'Bit of a new image thing going on,' said Herb. 'There's a few younger blokes come into it lately. They're good, too, can't knock 'em. They reckon the band wants to be more visual. Get into the pop group scene more – everyone leaping about in red knickerbockers. One of them's got a contact in the telly business, you see. Can't blame them, can you? Everyone aims at the big time. Only I'm not much cop at the leaping about.' Pip flushed with fury at the injustice of this and Herb went on quickly: 'They've been very decent about it. Said I was welcome to sit in whenever it was just sound. They're hoping to put a dem. tape together soon.'

There was a pause. Pip stared at the Aga wretchedly. He knew Herb would not want sympathy. It just made it worse.

'You got to face facts,' said Herb. 'I'm getting to be a right old heap of rubbish.' He nodded at the bed which stood in the corner of the room beside the trunk with its open lid and added: 'I'll never get upstairs again. Not that it matters.'

After an even longer pause, Pip said: 'Would you like some tea?'

'Good idea,' said Herb.

Spooning tea into the pot, Pip asked the question he had never put to Herb, though he had often thought of it. 'Do your legs hurt? I mean, a lot?'

'Yes,' said Herb. He leaned his head against the back of his chair in the attitude familiar to Pip, and shut his eyes as he had done when playing the trumpet. Then he opened them and gave a short laugh. 'Still,' he said, 'we're not immortal, thank God.'

'You mustn't die!' exclaimed Pip, and hot water from the kettle hissed across the top of the Aga as he missed the teapot.

'Steady on,' said Herb. 'Don't scald yourself, Buddy, or you'll never play the trumpet. You don't have to worry, I'll always be around. You know,' he added, 'you're getting to play quite well. You're going to be pretty good.'

'Really?' Pip forgot Herb's troubles in his delight.

'Main thing is to keep at it,' said Herb. 'What's the music like at this education palace you go to?'

'Pretty good, I think,' said Pip. 'Mr Bennett's a laugh, but he doesn't let anyone muck about. And they've got a brass band and an orchestra and a choir.'

'Good,' said Herb. 'Because you're going to need a proper teacher.'

'But –' began Pip.

'Oh, I know, there's always me,' agreed Herb. 'But you're going to need someone else. You must ask at school about it.' He went on quickly before Pip could interrupt. 'You need to play with other people.'

'Oh,' said Pip. This was a new idea.

Unusually, Herb leaned forward and ruffled Pip's hair. 'Cheer up, Buddy Bickerstaff,' he said. 'It'll be all right, you'll see. Now, where's this tea?'

'Coming,' said Pip.

It was late by the time Pip got home and he walked into a family rumpus. Geoff had come storming downstairs in his dressing-gown to point out that he couldn't be expected to get up at five and do his milk round if he was prevented from sleeping at night by people coming and going as if the place was a road-house. Nobody took any notice. Kevin was kissing a girl with pink hair on the sofa and Janice and Meryl were quarrelling over who had said what to cause Dennis to hit Allan at the disco. Edna came in and said she had won three quid and a fluffy mat to go round the toilet seat so she was happy.

'Bloody capitalism!' shouted Geoff. 'That's what it is! You're all its slaves!' He pounced on Pip, who was trying to sneak up to bed unnoticed. 'And you,' he demanded. 'Where have *you* been?'

'Round at Uncle Herb's,' said Pip.

'Just wait till I see him in the morning,' said Geoff. 'He'll get a piece of my mind along with his pint. And I hope you're finding time for your homework. Education is the hope of the masses.'

'If you weren't so busy with your bloody mice,' said Edna, 'you'd *know* if he was doing his homework. Now, all you lot can shut up, because I'm going to bed.'

For some days after that Geoff took an oppressive interest in Pip's homework and he had no opportunity to go and see Herb. During the weekly music lesson at school he found an opportunity to ask Mr Bennett about trumpet lessons and found that tuition was indeed available. Pip resolved to go and tell Herb about it straight after supper. He only had French homework tonight, and he could do that as soon as he got home. But as school ended and bikes and buses and walkers were pouring out of the school gate, Pip saw his father standing on the opposite pavement, his hands thrust into his mac pockets and a sheaf of papers tucked untidily under his arm.

'There's your old man,' said Micky Beales, grinning. 'You going to help him hand out leaflets?'

'No, I'm *not*,' said Pip. And by keeping a slow-moving bus between himself and Geoff, he managed to get out of the gate unnoticed, and ducked down the footpath which led to the bridge over the canal. It was a longer way home but one which he often took. He paused on the iron footbridge and looked down at the slowly gliding water. It wasn't like the sea, but it was oddly comforting. And tonight he would see

Herb. He walked home, whistling.

His mother looked up as he came into the kitchen. 'Didn't you see your father?' she asked.

'Where?' asked Pip innocently.

Edna's face creased with annoyance. 'Trust him to muck it up,' she said.

Pip made for the hall door. He would have the bedroom to himself until Kevin got home at half-past six. 'I've just got a bit of French,' he said, 'then I want to go round to Uncle Herb's. He said –'

'You can't,' said Edna flatly.

'But –'

Pip's protest died in his throat as his mother stubbed out a half-smoked cigarette, sat down on the sofa and patted the seat beside her. 'Come and sit down, love,' she said.

Something was wrong. Something was terribly wrong. With leaden legs, Pip moved back across the room and sat on the edge of the sofa.

'Now, you know Uncle Herb's never been well, don't you?' began his mother kindly. Pip nodded. 'Well, he's been getting worse lately,' Edna went on. 'Not really able to get about. Geoff's noticed it. He always kept an eye on Herb, see, when he dropped the milk in for him in the mornings. He went down to the school to meet you – I can't think how you missed him.'

Pip clenched his fists and tucked them between his knees. The dread which was mounting inside him made the room seem hot.

Edna sighed and said irritably, 'You've got to know sooner or later. I can't make it easy for you.' She put her hand on Pip's arm and pushed it gently a couple of times as if she was rocking him. Then she said, 'Uncle Herb's dead, Pip. He wasn't in the house this morning when your dad called with the milk so he thought something must be wrong. He couldn't go far, you see, just down the garden.'

Pip nodded again. He kept swallowing hard but the tears

were trickling down his face.

'They found him in the canal,' said his mother. 'This afternoon. That's what your father came to tell you.'

Pip bolted to the door and groped his way blindly upstairs to throw himself on his bed, choking with sobs. There was nowhere to go now. And Herb – even to himself he could hardly bear to frame the thought in words – Herb would not play the trumpet any more.

The door opened. 'Look,' said Edna awkwardly, 'don't take on so, love. I know you were fond of him, but you couldn't wish him to stay alive if he didn't want to. It's a happy release, really.'

From downstairs, Geoff's voice came plaintively. 'Edna! I waited until they'd all gone, but he wasn't there. I went to see the Headmaster in case the little bugger's been playing truant, but he hadn't. Quite an interesting chap, old Blanchard. Surprisingly Left for a Headmaster.'

Edna muttered something under her breath, paused irresolutely as she looked at her weeping son then, at a repeated call of 'Edna!', went downstairs.

For the next few days, everything seemed like a bad dream. Pip was dazed with misery. Kevin, seeing his brother's white face, rubbed out the chalk line which divided their shared room into two territories and gave him a speedometer off an old Triumph. Meryl refrained from referring to Herb as 'that old freak' and Janice said her boyfriend would take Pip fishing one Saturday if he liked. None of it helped. And then Geoff came back from seeing the solicitor with a large cardboard box in his hands. 'I don't hold with inherited wealth,' he said, 'but Herb left you this, Pip.'

Inside the box was Herb's trumpet and the stack of music. There was a note with it, written in pencil. 'My trumpet and the music are for my nephew, Philip Bickerstaff. I'll be around, Buddy. Signed, Herbert Bickerstaff.'

Pip was plunged into another long fit of weeping, and

could not bring himself to touch the trumpet.

The next day was the funeral.

In a weird sort of way, Pip rather liked the cemetery. It stood on rising ground just past the sewage works and rooks flapped and cawed in the tall trees at its edge. It was November now, and the sky was grey and wind-torn. Geoff had insisted on wearing Wellingtons but the women skirted the puddles on the gravel paths distastefully, and stood awkwardly balanced on the duckboards which the undertakers had provided round the open grave. The coffin, Pip thought, seemed to have nothing to do with Herb. It was as ominous as a bomb, with its long, tapering shape and its fearful neatness, and yet its brass handles were reminiscent of something cosier – a blanket chest, perhaps, or a coal scuttle.

Geoff, who was obstinately wearing a red tie instead of a black one, saying that Herb would have understood the principle at stake, folded his arms and stared at the distant trees in order to express his dissociation from the Vicar's words as the service began. Religion, he often said, was the opium of the people.

Pip tried hard not to think about Herb. It had begun to seem that the important thing now was to find something to hang on to. Somewhere, almost lost within him, there was still the feeling of space; of a different way of being. It was something to do with the scudding grey clouds and with his dream about the sea; an almost painful yearning which was at its strongest when he stared from his bedroom window across the imprisoning roofs and wished he could see the canal with its shining, moving water. 'That's your immortal soul, Buddy,' Herb had said. But no. That was dangerous ground. Pip scowled at the long mound of earth which stood ready beside the very deep, straight-sided hole. He must not cry again. The earth was covered with a cloth of artificial grass like they used on the fruit stalls in the market. How ludicrous. Did these burial people think the sight of earth was upsetting?

Despite this rational thought, tears were very close. Suddenly Pip noticed a small brown dog trotting in a purposeful way between the gravestones. It was a graceless animal, rough and perky, with a tail carried in a cheeky upward curve. Pip watched it as it approached the group of people standing round the open grave. 'My shoes are bloody ruined,' Janice was murmuring to Meryl. The dog seemed to find the pile of earth interesting. It sniffed carefully at the corner of the artificial grass then, turning sideways, raised a leg and directed a brief jet of urine over it, then trotted away. Even in the midst of his grief, Pip smiled.

'That's better,' said Herb.

Pip gasped. The voice was as close as he had ever heard it. His uncle was standing beside him. But there was nothing to be seen.

'Don't let on,' Herb warned him. 'They'll make an awful fuss.'

'I can't believe it!' said Pip. Everyone looked round reproachfully and Meryl said. 'Shut up.'

'I told you not to let on,' said Herb. 'They won't like it. Good thing about the dog. You were so busy being miserable, I couldn't get to you. I told you I'd be around.'

'I didn't understand,' whispered Pip, and incurred more disapproving looks.

'I'll see you back home,' said Herb. 'Only make things worse if I stick around here.'

Pip nodded. The men were paying out the long ropes which supported the coffin, lowering it into the ground. The dog had disappeared.

A surprising number of relatives and neighbours congregated in the Bickerstaffs' front room for drinks and sandwiches. There were Geoff's fellow mouse-fanciers and Edna's Bingo friends and a lot of cousins and aunts. All Kevin's mates arrived, mostly on bikes, and Janice's boyfriend brought the lads from the garage where he worked. Meryl said she thought it was a bit much, because she'd only asked Andrea and all that lot.

The afternoon wore on and everyone got drunker. The wind had dropped and a fitful winter sun came out. The mouse fanciers went out to the shed with Geoff to compare notes on his stock, and Kevin's mates straggled into the yard to do something to a bike. The remaining people slumped in the sitting-room and on the stairs and draped themselves about in the kitchen-dinette. Conversation became desultory. Apart from the occasional revving of a convalescent motor bike, the house was quiet. And upstairs in his bedroom, Pip raised the trumpet to his lips and began to play 'Buddy Bolden's Blues.'

'That's nice,' said Edna, idly tapping her feet in their mud-stained shoes. 'On the telly, is it?' But Geoff came bursting in from the mouse shed, his eyes bulging behind their glasses. 'Listen to that!' he said. 'Good grief, I thought it was Herb! I didn't know the boy could play like that – sends shivers down your spine, doesn't it!'

'It's nice,' said Edna again. 'I was thinking about Pip on the way back from the funeral,' she added placidly. 'There's a lot of Herb about him, really. The way he walks, even. Only he's lucky, he's got two good legs.'

People were congregating in the yard, staring up at the open window where Pip stood, his head back and his eyes closed as he played. He and Herb, through lips and mind and lungs and fingers, were totally absorbed in the music. The sea stretched from his feet to the horizon, sparkling and calm, and the feeling of space was tremendous. It did not matter that he could not see the canal.

THREE

The Fire Escape

Ever since they had come to this house, Lindsay had been lonely. This evening he stared out of his bedroom window at the bleak view below him. The early winter dusk was falling and the roar of rush-hour traffic drifted up from the streets. A few leaves still clung to the plane tree in the back garden but Lindsay could see between its branches to the landscape of roofs and chimneys which lay beyond the railway track.

Between the railway and the dilapidated fence at the end of the garden was an area of waste land. A fire was burning down there, and people were crouched round it. Not very many, four or five; perhaps. In the fading light, Lindsay could not be sure. He saw the gleam of a bottle as it was passed from one hand to another. The people were always there. Lindsay envied them. At least they had each other.

'Terrific potential,' Lindsay's father had said when they came to the tall, narrow London house, 'Lots of scope for improvement.' Lindsay missed the rambling cottage in Lincolnshire, and missed the friends he had made there. He could not get used to the idea that the house was sandwiched between two others, pressed tightly from either side like someone jammed in a crowded lift. His bedroom was at the top of the house so that, lying in bed, he could only see sky through the sash window. Beside it was a door which led out onto the fire escape.

The fire escape was black and spindly, zig-zagging down the outside of the building like a folding foot rule in fancy dress. Lindsay liked it. He had chosen this room because of it. The iron treads were punched with a lattice of diamond-shaped holes and, looking down through them, the earth seemed a long way below. The ricketty structure made a tremendous clanging noise if you ran down it quickly, and the whole thing quivered. Bits of rust kept falling off it. The concrete slab underneath it was stained a dark orange because of the rust and the rain.

Lindsay's mother hated the fire escape. 'It's so ugly,' she said. 'And so frightfully high up. I don't like the thought of Lindsay going out onto it from his room. Suppose there was an accident? I think we ought to keep that door locked.' Lindsay's father had pointed out that emergency exit doors were useless unless they were open. 'Fire regulations,' he said pompously, and his wife did not argue. She never argued, but she sighed and shook her head whenever she saw Lindsay clattering down the iron steps.

A handbell clanged several times from downstairs. That would be tea, Lindsay thought. 'Coming!' he shouted, but without any hope of being heard. There were four floors between him and the basement kitchen which the family found the cosiest room in the house; that was why his mother had instituted the handbell. But the melancholy of the winter evening filled him with depression and he continued to lean his elbows on the window-sill, staring out at the flickering bonfire.

'Go along, Master William.'

The voice was close behind him, chiding and intimate. Lindsay jumped round. The room was empty. 'Who is it?' he whispered.

'Don't keep your mother waiting, there's a good boy.' It was a woman's voice, cosy and slightly lisping. The back of Lindsay's neck felt prickly. He stared round the empty room, telling himself that he was just excited, not really frightened. And anyway, being scared was better than being lonely. He cleared his throat bravely and asked, 'Are you a ghost?'

'Ask no questions and you'll be told no lies,' said the voice smugly. 'Now, run along or Nanny will be cross.'

'But I want to know,' Lindsay insisted. '*Are* you?'

There was silence in the room and the bell clanged again from downstairs. Lindsay waited, half fearing and half hoping to hear the voice of the unseen woman again – but the silence continued. He opened the door to the fire escape and went out.

There was a dull orange glow from the streets and in the gaps between houses he could see the traffic like a moving necklace of headlights. The fire still burned on the waste land and a shower of sparks flew up as someone threw on some more wood. Probably planks from their garden fence, Lindsay thought. His father was always grumbling about it. Lit by the leaping flames, the faces round the fire shone white, like skulls. Lindsay gave a shiver. He glanced over his shoulder at the dark window of his room, and shivered again. Then he ran down the iron steps to the kitchen.

'There's a ghost in my room!' he announced proudly. 'It was talking to me!' He was determined not to be afraid of it.

His mother, turning the crumpets on the grill, looked at him with a troubled frown. 'I know you're a bit lonely here,' she said, 'but you mustn't start imagining things.'

'But there *is*!' Lindsay insisted. His mother pursed her lips as she slid the grill pan back, and he felt his excitement contract inside him, tucking itself away like a small glow of light at the back of his mind. He gave a little sigh. 'I was only joking,' he said. He went to the bench seat beside the scrubbed pine table and sat down with his hands clenched between his knees, waiting for the crumpets to be done.

The next day, Lindsay brought Gary home after school. He was not sure that he liked Gary but his mother worried about him not making friends. Gary sat next to Lindsay in Art, where they shared a dislike of painting 'A Winter Scene',

Lindsay because he considered the subject old-fashioned, and Gary because he thought it was soppy.

'You live in Arcot Street? That's where all them old meths drinkers hang out, innit?' said Gary, as he and Lindsay made their way back from the underground station.

'I had a model steam engine once,' said Lindsay, 'and that ran on meths. I didn't know you could drink it, though.'

'You can't,' said Gary. 'Drives you bonkers. The old down-and-outs drink it if they can't afford anything else. Let's go round the back and see if they're about. Always good for a laugh.'

'Mum will get into a tizz if I'm late,' said Lindsay rather feebly. He did not want to go round whatever back Gary had in mind, but he knew he must not appear to be a coward.

'Won't kill her to wait for ten minutes,' said Gary. 'Mine used to make an awful fuss but she got used to it. Come on.' He turned down a concrete alley beside a block of flats and broke into a run. Lindsay had to run as well, to keep up with him. The clatter of their footsteps rang back from the high concrete walls. They came out into a litter-strewn area of muddy grass flanked by the remains of wooden seats, most of whose slats had been torn off, and went through a gap in an old brick wall which looked as if it had once been part of something else. They came out on the waste land beside the railway.

'That's my house,' said Lindsay, pointing across to the unfamiliar view of the back of the Georgian terrace. 'The one that hasn't been painted white or pink yet.'

'The one with the falling-down fence?' asked Gary.

'Yes,' said Lindsay. 'Dad says he'll mend it, but he wants to finish stripping the doors first.' He was suddenly rather enviously aware that Gary's parents would never dream of buying a house with terrific potential. He shifted his gaze. 'That's where they have their bonfire,' he said, 'over there beside that –' He stopped short, staring.

'Beside that heap of old rags?' Gary supplied. Then he,

too, stared. 'Hang on,' he said, and began to pick his way forward across the rubble and broken bottles. Reluctantly, Lindsay followed. Then they both stopped.

'It isn't a pile of old rags,' Lindsay whispered.

'It's a gonner,' said Gary. 'A corpse, Cor, smashing.' But his voice was a little unsteady and he made no move to look more closely.

'It might be somebody ill,' reasoned Lindsay, trying to still the panic which had swept over him. He went a little closer. There was no movement from the inert figure beside the ashes of the burned-out bonfire. It lay on its side, knees drawn up under the old black overcoat, the arms crossed so that the hands were tucked between the coat and its sleeves for warmth. A man's felt hat, dark and greasy, covered part of the face but Lindsay saw with horror that the skin was puckered and scarred. Most of the nose had at some time been burned away, leaving the nostril as a dark, gaping hole. The scarred chin was beardless and long, grey hair straggled over the hunched shoulders.

'It's a woman,' said Lindsay. In horrified fascination, he bent over the still body. It smelt like the stale reek which came up from the pub cellar when the doors on the pavement were open to let the men lower new barrels into it, but dirty as well, musty and sharp. Then Lindsay gasped. An eye had opened in the puckered, grimy face. Black and malevolent, it glared up at him as the toothless mouth clamped shut then opened again as if it was thirsty. Lindsay jumped back.

'What is it?' asked Gary, who had been watching from a safe distance.

'She's alive!' said Lindsay, and they both ran as if the old woman was a bomb which might go off at any moment.

'This way!' gasped Lindsay, veering aside to make for the fence at the bottom of his garden. They ducked through the gaps left by the missing planks, pelted across the over-grown grass and down the short flight of stone steps under the fire escape, and burst into the kitchen.

'Goodness!' said Lindsay's mother, looking up from her ironing board, 'What on earth's the matter?'

'Nothing,' panted Lindsay, trying to look casual.

'Just had a race,' said Gary. He grinned at Lindsay sheepishly and Lindsay grinned back, knowing that Gary, too, was wondering why they had taken to their heels in such panic. The woman was only an old down-and-out. She couldn't hurt them. And yet, in that moment when Lindsay had found himself looked at by that beady black eye, so horribly alive in the ugly face, he had been terrified.

'Why don't you two go and play upstairs?' suggested Lindsay's mother. 'Just while I finish the ironing. I was getting quite worried about you, being so late back, but it's nice you've found a friend. Can you stay for tea – er – er – I don't know your name, do I?'

'Gary,' said Gary. 'Yes, please. Smashing.'

Lindsay took Gary up the fire escape to his room, despite a pained glance from his mother. He could tell by the way Gary stamped up the iron treads that he liked it.

'Here we are,' said Lindsay. He opened the door to his room and switched on the light.

'Great,' said Gary. He glanced round at the faded wall-paper and the iron fire surround with a gas fire behind a brass fender. 'Bit old-fashioned, innit?' he asked.

'My parents like old-fashioned things,' said Lindsay defensively.

Gary grinned. 'I seen a play on telly where there was a room like this. About a kid who had a nanny what hit him with a slipper. Right old bat she was. Skinny. Wore a black dress with buttons down the front.'

'Oh, yes,' agreed Lindsay. 'There's one of those here.'

'Whatcher mean?' asked Gary.

Lindsay blushed. It had been a silly thing to say. 'I mean, I expect there was,' he said quickly. 'You could imagine there was.'

'Yeah,' said Gary. He grinned again. 'What about the old

bird out there, then? Gave you a turn, didn't she?'

'I like that!' protested Lindsay. 'You didn't even come close enough to look!'

'Them old dossers can get quite nasty,' said Gary with dignity. 'If you got any sense, you don't get near enough so's they can grab you.' He embarked on a long series of tales about dossers and their habits and Lindsay listened, fascinated. Like a small pain, the thought of the woman in a black dress nagged at him. She was not skinny, as Gary had said. He had seen her last night when he was in bed, just dozing off to sleep, and she was quite fat. She had thick wrists. But then, Gary had only seen some silly television programme; he couldn't be expected to know. Lindsay toyed briefly with the idea of telling Gary about it, and decided not to. Gary would laugh.

Lindsay's father moved the blowlamp flame slowly down a cream-painted door panel. 'Time you were in bed,' he said without looking round.

Lindsay didn't answer. He had been thinking hard since tea.

'Yes, run along, dear,' said his mother.

'Actually,' Lindsay ventured, 'I was going to ask if I could swop my bedroom.'

'Not *now*?' enquired his mother, pained.

'Some time,' said Lindsay. 'If I could just – swop.'

The scraper gave a long, shrill squeal as Lindsay's father shaved off the newly-blistered paint. 'You made your choice,' he said. 'Now stick to it.' He applied the blowlamp to the next area of paint.

'But –' began Lindsay.

'You heard what your father said,' his mother reproved him. 'Now, off you go. And not up the fire escape.'

Lindsay reluctantly did as he was told. There was a kind of mounting dread about going up the lino-clad stairs. The brass edgings with their worn criss-cross grooves were somehow sinister, and so was the dark wallpaper, although its pattern of brown leaves was interrupted by stark white streaks where the new wiring had been chanelled into the walls. He wished he had not brought Gary home. The casual reference to a woman in a black dress had brought the strange presence in Lindsay's bedroom a big step further forward. It was as though, without realising it, Gary too had known that the woman was there. Until now, Lindsay had been able to persuade himself that it had just been a dream last night. But it had seemed so real. The owner of the cosy voice was a solid, bulky woman; and yet there had been something different about her. Underlying the cosiness was something impatient and angry. Something frightening.

Lindsay sat on his bed and glared round at the mauve-striped wallpaper with its knots of roses. 'You just stay away,' he said fiercely. 'Do you hear?' And in the same instant he tingled with shame, as if he had been slapped for his cheekiness.

He got up defiantly and went to the window. He was aware that the unseen presence was watching him but he tried to look casual. Down on the waste land, the fire burned. Lindsay thought of the woman who looked like a pile of rags and remembered the toothless mouth in the scarred face, and the black, accusing eye. He shuddered. And behind him, close enough to make the hair on his scalp crawl, there was a dry, unpleasant chuckle. He would not let himself turn round. If she was there, he did not want to see her. But at last the feeling that he was not alone overwhelmed him and he spun round with a gasp of terror. The mauve-striped wallpaper mocked him with its emptiness.

Lindsay tried to stay awake that night. He stared with prickling, wide-open eyes at the ceiling, where a faint shifting of the light reminded him that the bonfire still burned. It's all right, he thought determinedly. I'm still awake. She can't come. She only comes when I'm dropping off to sleep. But the comfort of that thought brought with it a warm, fatal relaxation and the hands were there before him, clasped in front of the black, silky fabric, smug and white and threatening. The voice was as quiet as a confidential whisper. 'Master William,' it said, 'you were a wicked boy today. You disturbed me.'

Lindsay wanted to protest that he was not William that it was all wrong. But he could make no sound. He stared at the hands and at the thick wrists tightly buttoned into the black sleeves. The line of small black buttons led up the bodice to the high collar, the roll of fat under the chin, the mouth clamped into a sagging line. And the black eyes stared down at him with the same hatred which had sent him running across the waste land that very afternoon.

'See what has become of me,' whispered the woman. 'I lost my position, Master William. All because of you.'

No, shouted Lindsay, you've got it wrong. But he made no sound.

'A little bit of comfort,' the lisping voice went on. 'That's all I wanted. But you had to interfere, Master William. You had to spoil it all.'

Lindsay shrank down in his bed and covered his face with his hands. The sleeves of his pyjamas felt tight on his wrists and he fingered a cuff cautiously, unable to understand what had happened. His curiosity overcame his fear and he opened his eyes. He found that he was wearing a white nightshirt, the full sleeves gathered into tight cuffs. This must be a dream, he told himself. But it did not feel like a dream.

Stealthily, he pulled the sheet down a little so that he could see out. The table beside his bed, usually bare except for his books and his alarm clock, was covered by a dark green chenille cloth with a fringe of bobbles round the edge. On it stood a brass oil lamp, burning with a steady yellow flame. Across the room, the woman in a black dress sat by the coal fire in a rocking chair which creaked rhythmically as she rocked to and fro, humming to herself. She held a small glass in her hand and a bottle stood in the fireplace, its neck just visible above the brass fender. She drained the contents of the glass and reached forward for the bottle, glancing across at the bed as she did so. She frowned when she saw the boy watching her.

Instinctively, Lindsay flinched at the scrutiny of the black eyes, remembering with someone else's mind that he had been savagely punished on previous occasions for seeing what he was not supposed to see. Once again, he covered his face with his hands.

'We going to have another look at the old dossers, then?' asked Gary after school the next day.

'No, we're not,' said Lindsay promptly. 'And you can't come home to tea today because Mum says I've got to go with her to get some new shoes.'

'Okay,' said Gary easily. 'Didn't ask, did I? Might as well go home your way, though.' He whistled loudly after a girl in high heels, and Lindsay blushed.

There was a shop on the corner of Arcot Street with milk crates stacked on the pavement outside it, and a litter bin overflowing with empty cans. Gary casually picked a Coke can out of the bin and tossed it ahead of him to kick noisily along the pavement. Lindsay ran to get a kick in as well and they made their way cheerfully down Arcot Street, pushing and barging at each other to get a turn in at kicking the can.

'Hey!' said Gary suddenly, 'Look!'

Ahead of them, a shapeless figure in a dirty black overcoat shuffled along the pavement. Grey hair straggled from under the battered hat and the bare, mauve-blotched legs ended in a gaping pair of army boots with no laces.

Lindsay stopped. 'It's her,' he said.

Gary grabbed the can, took a couple of quick steps and drop-kicked it at the shuffling figure. It hit the woman a glancing blow on the shoulder. She turned with surprising speed and let loose a stream of invective. Lindsay did not understand most of the words she used but their intention was unmistakeable. The old woman shook her fist in a passion of hatred and her face, contorted with loathing, was the face of Lindsay's waking dream.

Gary indicated Lindsay with a cheerful jerk of his thumb and shouted, 'He was the one what done it!'

'It wasn't!' protested Lindsay. He started to tell Gary what he thought of this calumny but the old woman stopped swearing and took a couple of purposeful steps towards them. Her black eyes blazed with fury.

'Come on!' said Gary, and took to his heels. It seemed an age to Lindsay before he could tear his gaze away from the black eyes. His feet felt leaden as he tried to run and each step was a painful jolt which clanged in his brain like the echo from high walls.

Lindsay left his light on that night, but his father came in and switched it off. 'No need to have the place lit up like the Blackpool illuminations,' he said. 'Costing me enough as it is, what with gas for the blowlamp. . . .' He went grumbling out.

In the dark, Lindsay lay with his fists clenched and his eyes wide open. The nameless threat seethed all round him as the light from the bonfire flickered faintly on the ceiling. I didn't do it, he said silently. I didn't throw the can. Honest. But he knew it was no good.

He stayed awake for a long time, lying as rigidly as a soldier at attention. He heard his parents go to bed in their room below his, and after a while he heard the click of their light being turned out. He ached from lying so stiffly on his back, and turned on his side to be more comfortable. It was much better like that. Warm . . . .

'So, Master William,' whispered the voice, very close to him. 'The wicked must be punished, must they not?' One plump finger tapped implacably on the back of the other hand.

'Please,' Lindsay begged. 'I didn't do it. I didn't.'

The plump fingers reached out and gripped him by the ear, twisting it mercilessly until he cried out with pain. Somewhere, a part of his mind was angry that he could make no sound. And then he was awake again, staring at the light on the ceiling. His ear was throbbing. I shouldn't have let myself go to sleep, he thought.

The light on the ceiling was concentrated in a circle, he noticed, a warm, yellow glow, much closer than the dim flicker of the bonfire. It was the light of an oil lamp. Oh, no. Horror flushed through his veins like cold water. He was awake; he was sure he was awake. But he was in the room of his dreams. Somebody was singing; a tuneless, moody song accompanied by the regular creak of the rocking chair. Furtively, Lindsay looked out. The woman clasped the bottle to the tight black silk of her bosom as she rocked by the fire. Her head turned restlessly from side to side against the back of the chair; her hair was escaping from its pins and dangled in grey-streaked locks across her shoulder. Her unfocussed gaze met Lindsay's and the black eyes were suddenly sharp. She stopped singing. She got up from the chair, lurched a little then recovered herself and advanced towards the bed, the bottle dangling by its neck from one hand.

'I told you before,' she said thickly, 'little boys who pry come to a bad end. My bit of comfort – nothing to do with you. You hear?' With her free hand, she shook Lindsay by the shoulder, digging her nails into his skin.

'Don't' he begged. 'You're hurting.' And as he spoke, he knew he was awake, for he could hear his own words.

'You must be punished,' she said. 'Nobody will hear if you scream. Your parents are out. I am in charge of you.'

'They're not out,' said Lindsay bravely. 'They're in bed. I heard them put their light out.' He sat up and pushed the bedclothes back.

'We are not going to be silly, are we, Master William?'

said the woman through tight lips. She stared at Lindsay until he subsided back onto the pillows, then, still looking at him, raised the bottle to her lips. She tilted her head back to drink, closing her eyes.

Lindsay seized his opportunity. He jumped out of bed and ran to the door. It would not open. He grappled desperately with the handle and heard the swish of silk as the woman came up behind him. Her fingers gripped him just above the elbow in a knowing pressure which made him scream out with the pain of it. But the scream was loud and real, and it was music in his ears. Despite the nightshirt he was wearing, despite the frowsty immediacy of the room and the coal fire burning in the grate, despite the awful presence of the woman, he was Lindsay and his real life was not this one. He wriggled round in the woman's grasp and kicked her hard on the shins.

'Ow!' she shrieked. 'You little devil!'

'Mummy!' yelled Lindsay. 'Daddy! Come up here, quickly! *Mummy*!'

The woman swung the bottle at him viciously but Lindsay ducked away, grabbing the bottle and twisting it out of her grasp. She swore at him and seized a handful of his hair. Lindsay's eyes watered with pain. He hurled the bottle into the fireplace so as to have both hands free to fend the woman off.

The bottle hit the edge of the grate and splintered into pieces. The woman gave a shriek of fury, released Lindsay and rushed to the fireplace just as flame broke out from the split spirit, licking across the fender. The woman swung round to scream abuse at Lindsay and the skirt of her black dress swirled out across the path of the flame. The silk flared up with terrifying speed.

Somebody was rattling at the door handle. The woman's dress was engulfed in flame. She beat at it with her hands, uselessly. Lindsay saw that the hearthrug was smouldering. The whole place was going to catch fire. And the door was locked. She probably had the key. Lindsay ran to the fire escape door and flung it open. The woman was close behind him, a human bonfire determined to engulf him in her flames. She grabbed him by the back of his nightshirt. He turned and pushed her away with all his strength. The black, burning, reeking weight of her body was impossibly heavy. 'No, Master William!' she shouted, 'You are coming with me!'

Lindsay found the outside wall of the house at his back, rough and cold and real. He leaned hard against it, thrusting the awful bulk of the woman away with a foot as well as both hands. There was a creaking, rending sound – and suddenly the weight fell away from him, down into the night air.

Lindsay stood on the iron platform at the top of the fire escape in his pyjamas, panting. And somebody panted beside him.

In cold terror, Lindsay turned his head. But it was somebody his own size who stood beside him, and it was a boy's voice which said, 'Thank you very much!' Brown eyes smiled into his, and dark hair curled over the high collar of the nightshirt. 'I've been stuck with that old horror for years.' the boy went on. 'And you've let me escape. *Thank* you.'

'You're William!' said Lindsay in astonishment.

' 'Sright!' said William. They grinned at each other. The rail in front of them gaped away into space, grotesquely twisted outwards. Then Lindsay heard footsteps running up towards him, and felt the iron platform quiver under his feet. Was it the woman? He shrank back into his room. William had gone. It was dark. There was no fire, no oil lamp. He switched on the light and clenched his fists, waiting.

'Good God!' said the voice outside. 'Look at that rail!' It was Lindsay's father.

Lindsay sat down on his bed and began to shiver. His father came into the room, his face almost comic in its consternation. 'Why on earth did you lock the door?' he demanded. Lindsay's mother pushed past her husband. 'Oh darling, are you all right?' she asked, running across to kneel beside Lindsay. 'Whatever happened?'

Lindsay felt terribly cold. 'Did you see her?' he asked. His parents glanced at each other. 'The woman in a black dress,' Lindsay persisted. 'She caught fire.'

'Nothing to do with fire, old chap,' said his father gently. 'The rail gave way on the fire escape and she fell through. She's – she's down there.'

'Is she dead?' asked Lindsay. Again, his parents looked at each other uneasily. '*Is* she?' demanded Lindsay.

'Yes, darling,' said his mother. 'I'm afraid she is.'

Lindsay nodded. 'That's what I thought,' he said. He fished under his bed for his slippers and put them on, then went across to the door to take his dressing-gown off the hook. A thought occurred to him and he tried the handle. The door opened. 'It wasn't locked,' he said calmly as he put on his dressing-gown.

'It jolly well was!' said his father hotly. His wife put out a restraining hand. 'Lindsay, what are you going to do?' she asked as her son tied his dressing-gown cord firmly and pushed his hands into his pockets.

'I'm going to look,' said Lindsay, and made determinedly for the fire escape. His mother gave a shriek of dismay. 'The rail! Oh, do come away!'

'It's all right,' Lindsay assured her as he started down the iron steps. He smiled to himself as he made his way down in the cold night air. A little thing like a broken rail was nothing to be afraid of. Beside him, William smiled as well.

The body huddled on the concrete slab looked at first glance like a pile of rags. The light from the basement kitchen shone across the putty-coloured face and the out-flung hands. The toothless mouth gaped and the grey hair straggled into a still-spreading pool of blood. Lindsay stooped and gazed steadily into the open black eye. It stared at nothing and its spark of hatred was gone.

William gave a little sigh of relief and Lindsay felt a surge of happiness. Then, quite unexpectedly, there came a kind of anguish for the crumpled body which had been a person and, more, for whatever nameless thing had made that person so terrible. He found that he was crying. William crouched beside him, his face anxious. 'It's all right,' he said. 'It isn't your fault, you see. You're just the person who had to do it.'

Lindsay's mother swept him into the kitchen, wrapped him in a blanket and sat him by the Aga while her husband phoned the police.

They had to bring the body through the terraced house to reach the ambulance standing at the front door. Lindsay glanced at the shapeless heap under the red blanket as the men carried the stretcher through. William waved goodbye to it and Lindsay smiled into his cocoa. His mother looked at him curiously. 'I – I was just thinking what Gary will say,' he invented rather wildly.

'Yes, quite a story to tell him,' said his mother. 'I'm so glad you're making friends.'

Lindsay nodded dutifully and smiled again. His friend was not Gary.

The policeman who had been talking to Lindsay's father closed his notebook and stood up. 'That's all we need for now,' he said. 'Thank you very much for your co-operation. And for the cocoa.'

'Who was she?' asked Lindsay's mother. 'Have you any idea?'

The policeman smiled briefly as he buttoned his notebook into his tunic pocket. 'The ambulance chaps know her of old,' he said. 'Been brought in drunk countless times. Sarah Hodden. Old Sal, they called her. She used to work in this house, you know – donkey's years ago. She was a nanny. But the parents came home one night to find the place in flames. The little chap she looked after was screaming blue murder. He blurted out some story about there being a struggle, but he was very badly burned. He died a few days later.'

'How awful!' said Lindsay's mother. William made a face at Lindsay and shrugged cheerfully.

'Pity it wasn't the old woman who died,' said Lindsay's father. 'It would have saved everyone a lot of trouble.'

'I don't think she ever worked again,' said the policeman. 'The fire left her face in a mess – enough to give any kid nightmares. She just became a down-and-out.'

'Certainly not the sort of person you'd employ as a nanny,' Lindsay's father agreed. He glanced at his wife but she was frowning inattentively. 'I can't think why she came back,' she said.

'Trying to burgle the place, I expect,' said Lindsay's father. 'But thanks to Lindsay scaring her off, she didn't get away with it. Not that I'd wish such a ghastly accident on anyone,' he added hastily.

'I think it's rather sad,' said Lindsay's mother. 'Poor old thing – perhaps she was wandering in her mind and thought the little boy was still here. She might have seen Lindsay and confused him with the boy she used to look after. I wonder what his name was.'

'William,' said Lindsay.

Everyone looked at him and William said: 'You are a twit, Lindsay.'

'I mean,' Lindsay amended quickly, 'it *might* have been William.' He yawned in an off-hand sort of way.

'Back to bed,' said his mother firmly. She turned to her husband and added, 'We *can* let him change his bedroom tomorrow, can't we? After what happened tonight –'

'Of course we can,' said Lindsay's father benevolently. 'That's the great thing about a house like this, there's plenty of room. Stacks of potential.'

Lindsay shook his head. 'Oh, no,' he said. 'It's quite all right now. I like that room, really I do.'

'William nodded. 'So do I,' he said.

Lindsay smiled as they all stared at him dubiously. They were so funny, looking through William as if he wasn't there.

'I'll go to bed now,' he told them, and opened the door to the hall. He wouldn't suggest going up the fire escape. Not tonight. They would only be upset.

He smiled again at their puzzled faces and closed the door gently behind him. Then he started up the lino-covered stairs, whistling. His shadow zig-zagged across the brown leaves on the wallpaper. William, whistling beside him noisily, cast no shadow, but he grinned at Lindsay as they reached the first floor and started up the next flight of stairs. 'Race you!' he said, and they pelted side by side up through the narrow house to the empty, welcoming bedroom.

FOUR

Photographs

Ruth climbed the seventh flight of concrete stairs to Mrs Barton's flat, having stopped off at the fifth for Mr Cartwright. She was out of breath and the foil-lined cardboard containers of food she carried were uncomfortably hot.

Ruth rang the bell and waited. The door opened just as she was extending her finger to ring again. 'Hello,' she said to Mrs Barton. 'Meals on Wheels.'

The old woman stared at Ruth suspiciously from sagging, colourless eyes. She was very fat and her blue jersey was stretched tightly across her stomach, making her look like a toddler growing out of his clothes. 'Who are you?' she asked.

'I'm Ruth Astey,' said Ruth. 'I'm helping my mother with the Meals on Wheels. It's the school holidays, you see.' And she was doing a project on 'Old People in the Community' for her sociology course, but there didn't seem much point in trying to explain that to Mrs Barton. 'Can I come in?' she added. 'These are awfully hot.'

Mrs Barton stood back a little reluctantly. Her hands and the lower part of her face wobbled slightly all the time, Ruth noticed, and she smelt. In fact, the whole flat smelt. It was awful. Like concentrated old face flannels, Ruth thought, sweetish and rotten and soft. It was terribly hot in the small living-room. Despite the sunny day, a gas fire glowed with incandescent heat. 'Where shall I put these?' she asked, indicating the containers of food. There did not seem to be a surface anywhere which was not cluttered with stuff – old stockings, newspapers and books, an open pot of jam, photographs and half-eaten packets of biscuits. Mrs Barton pushed vaguely at the things on the table, clearing a small space. 'I don't know you,' she said.

'That's right,' Ruth agreed, sliding the containers on to the table. 'You usually see my Mum. It's fish pie today, and lemon sponge. Have you got a plate ready, and a knife and fork?'

'You can leave it there,' said Mrs Barton indifferently. She had picked up a dog-eared photograph from the clutter on the table and was smoothing it carefully between her trembling fingers. 'That's Billy,' she said.

Ruth looked. It was a very old photograph, brown and faded. A young man and a girl stood with their backs to a pier railing, smiling with eyes half shut in the bright sunshine. He wore an open-necked shirt with a scarf tucked into it and had one arm round the girl's shoulders. She clasped a handbag in front of her and turned her face a little towards the boy as if in shyness of the camera. Her dark hair was pinned into an elaborate mass which made her neck look very slender.

'He'll come for me one day,' said Mrs Barton.

Ruth remembered her Sociology project. 'Are they relatives of yours?' she asked.

Mrs Barton did not seem to understand the question. 'He went on that ship,' she said 'The *Empire Star*. He wrote to me. Lovely letters from Port Said and Singapore . . . lots of places. Then my father died and we had to move. Mother got a job as a governess. Sybil Davis, the girl was called. Then Eleanor Banbury – was it Banbury? There were so many. We moved about from house to house. I always wrote to Billy. Then the shipping company started sending my letters back. They said the *Empire Star* had been lost in the Indian Ocean. But Billy wasn't lost. I know Billy wasn't lost.'

'The girl in the photograph – you mean, it's you?' asked Ruth. Had the slim figure in the dress with long collars and a droopy bow really become this smelly mountain of flesh?

'That was before I had my hair cut,' explained

Mrs Barton. She smiled at the photograph and added: 'He'll be here any day now.'

Ruth's face was glowing with the stuffy heat and she realised that her mother would be waiting for her downstairs in the car. 'Mum said you'd have the money ready,' she said apologetically. She had not got over her embarrassment about asking the old people to pay for their meals.

'Bag,' said Mrs Barton vaguely, looking round the room. She shuffled out to the kitchenette in her slippers with the trodden-down heels and Ruth, left alone, stared again at the photograph of Billy and the girl who had become Mrs Barton. Had Billy really gone down with the *Empire Star*? He might have changed ships, she thought, unwilling to believe that the smiling boy was dead. Or perhaps he had stayed in port somewhere because he was ill. Or the old girl might have got it all wrong and the sailor was Billy Barton, the man she had married. There was another photograph on the mantelpiece, a framed portrait of a young man with carefully-brushed hair and a grave expression. He looked very young and very serious, like a dog that had been put on trust to guard his master's possessions. And, Ruth thought, he seemed sad. His eyes had a look of resignation, as if he had learned to live without hoping for anything.

Mrs Barton came back, rummaging in a dilapidated handbag. She found her purse and counted out the money painstakingly.

'Thank you,' said Ruth. The sad young man whose face gazed out so gravely from the mantelpiece caught her eye again and she asked: 'Is that Billy, too?'

'Oh, no,' said Mrs Barton. 'That's Arthur.' She frowned at the photograph for a moment and her face quivered more violently. 'I couldn't help marrying Arthur,' she said. 'He did love me so much and everyone said the *Empire Star* had gone down. But it's all right now. Arthur was only for a time. Billy can come whenever he wants to now.' She stared into Ruth's face with sudden intensity and Ruth saw with revulsion that a small dribble of saliva was running from the corner of her mouth. 'You will tell him, won't you?' she said. 'I think – I won't be able to. You must tell him.'

'My mother will be waiting –' Ruth began uneasily, but the old woman seized her by the wrist and tugged her towards the table. 'You must take this,' she insisted, and thrust the seaside photograph into Ruth's hand. 'Then you will know Billy when you see him. You must tell him – Elsie still loves him. He can come now, whenever he wants.'

Ruth looked at Mrs Barton in alarm. The old woman's face was a bluish purple and she was breathing heavily. 'I think you'd better sit down,' Ruth said gently.

Mrs Barton lowered herself into a chair, wheezing slightly. She waved a dismissive, shaking hand at Ruth and whispered: 'Tell him.'

'I will,' Ruth promised. And, with the tattered photograph in one hand and Mrs Barton's dinner money in the other, she let herself out.

'Where on earth have you been?' demanded Ruth's mother as she sat in the car with the engine running.

'I'm sorry,' Ruth gasped. 'The lift is out of order, and she kept talking. It's really awfully weird, Mum –'

'Look, Ruth, you can't get involved with these old people,' said her mother, pulling away from the kerb. 'If you stop and talk to one you're keeping all the others waiting, and some of them think of their Meals on Wheels as the high point of their day. They get quite fretful if you're late.'

'Yes. I'm sorry I was so long,' said Ruth. 'I didn't *mean* to talk to her. But she started on about this boy called Billy – look, she gave me his photograph.'

'*Did* she?' Mrs Astey spared a momentary eye from the road to glance at the photograph in her daughter's hand. 'How very odd. We all know about Elsie Barton's Billy-fantasy. He was drowned years ago, or very probably, anyway, and she married someone else. Had a perfectly normal life as far as anyone can see – no children but they seemed quite happy. Arthur died about a year ago and ever since then this fantasy has been getting worse. I'm surprised Elsie gave you that photograph, though. It's her most treasured possession.'

'I wish she hadn't,' said Ruth. She felt obscurely guilty. 'She wants me to give it to Billy,' she explained, 'but I can't. It makes me feel so awful.'

'Don't get involved,' repeated her mother. 'A lot of these old folk are confused in their minds and it's all too easy to believe their delusions are real.' She slowed down and added, 'Now for Mr Jacks. He's quite a different kettle of fish. Very with-it.' She stopped outside a neat bungalow whose clipped lawns were edged with lobelia and white stones, and opened the car door. 'You or me?' she asked.

'Oh, me, please,' said Ruth. 'I mean, there *is* this project and I –'

'Get on with it, then,' said her mother as she opened the boot. 'I'll do Miss Beresford across the road.'

'Right,' said Ruth. She pushed the seaside photograph into her cardigan pocket so as to have both hands free, and took a container from each of the stacks in the boot of the car. Then she went in through the gate of the bungalow. The front door opened as she walked up the path and an old man leaning on a stick called; 'Good morning!' He wore an open-necked shirt with a scarf tucked into it, and his white hair was as neatly clipped as the lawns in his garden. 'Got a new recruit, have they?' he said, smiling at Ruth and stepping back politely to let her come past him into the hall. Through an open door she glimpsed a small dining-room where a table standing in the bay window was covered with a white cloth. Gleaming cutlery was set in readiness, complete with a silver cruet and water in a glass jug.

'Is it still hot?' Mr Jacks enquired, indicating the packages Ruth carried, 'or should I put those in the oven for a few minutes? You are a little late today.'

'I think it's all right,' said Ruth. 'I'm awfully sorry about being late – the last lady kept me talking. Elsie Barton,' she added, feeling that Mr Jacks might have met her at some Old Folks' Outing or Christmas party.

'It feels quite nice and hot,' said Mr Jacks as he took the containers in his free hand. 'The plates are warm, anyway. I always put them in a low oven at ten past twelve. The money's on the window sill by the front door.' Leaning on his stick, he made his way to the dining room then turned and added, 'Elsie who?'

'Barton,' said Ruth, gathering up the coins.

'Never heard of her,' said Mr Jacks, and went on into the dining-room. Ruth opened the front door and a sudden gust of wind caught the curtains at the hall window, blowing them inwards and buffeting Ruth's curly hair. Outside, her mother hooted impatiently. 'Bye-bye!' Ruth called to Mr Jacks, and he called back, 'Goodbye, my dear! Thank you!' The sun had gone in and Ruth pulled her cardigan round her as she ran down the path to the car.

Ruth went up to her room after supper, intent on writing some notes for her sociology project while the details were still fresh in her mind. She got out her file and wrote, 'Meals on Wheels' at the top of a fresh sheet of paper, and underlined it. During the day she had realised after the first three or four visits that the names were going to be difficult to remember, so she had jotted each one down on the back of an old envelope her mother had found in the car's glove box. Now, feeling virtuous for being so well organised, Ruth fished in her cardigan pocket and pulled out the folded envelope. And in that moment she realised that the photograph of Elsie Barton and the young sailor should be there as well. And it was not.

Although she was alone, Ruth flushed with shame. A part of her mind must have known all day that the photograph had gone. Surely her fingers should have told her, each time she pushed the envelope into her pocket or took it out, that there should be another, shiny-sided piece of paper beside it? She ran through the day's events again in her mind, trying to remember with certainty when she last had the photograph. She had put it in her pocket so as to have her hands free to take the containers up the path to Mr Jacks' front door – she was certain of that. For the rest of the day, however, she had no idea whether the photo was still in her pocket or not. She frowned at the page in front of her. Apart from anything else, the old photograph would have made an effective illustration to her project. But there was more to it than that. Much more.

That night, Ruth had a complicated, worrying dream. She was carrying two Meals on Wheels packages through a strange town with high buildings on either side of the street. The buildings were honeycombed with stairways and passages and the Meals on Wheels lady had simply said, 'You know Arthur Barton, don't you? These are for him.' Suddenly Ruth was sure she had arrived at the right door. She opened it and found the young Elsie of the photograph sitting at a table in a bay window. The sailor sat beside her, with his arms round her, and they were kissing. The curtains were blowing inwards and there was a smell of the sea. The couple turned radiant faces towards Ruth as she came in and Billy said: 'You're the girl who brought the photograph. Thank you very much. We owe you our happiness.'

'But I didn't,' Ruth said. 'I lost it. I've been looking for it everywhere.' The pocket of her cardigan was shallow and she feared that the photograph had fallen out. The containers of food were hot in her hands. 'What have you done with Arthur?' she asked severely, remembering what her mother had said about not getting involved. 'This dinner is for him, and people get upset if you're late.' But Elsie and the young sailor were kissing each other again, and Ruth was back in the echoing stairways of the strange town.

She came to the bottom of the concrete steps and turned the corner. Something was crouched in the shadow. A dog? She bent down to see. It was brown and shaggy and huddled, and it had the anxious, earnest face of Arthur Barton. 'What are you doing here?' cried Ruth, absurdly conscious that the packages of food she carried did not belong in the same world as this pitiful man-dog. Waves of sadness emanated from the creature and yet its face was quite calm. Ruth tried again. 'Where do you live?' she asked. 'I've got to deliver the Meals on Wheels and there's one for you.' A car hooted impatiently outside. Ruth did not want to go. She turned away reluctantly and when she looked back she saw that the man-dog was following her. It crept to her heels and lay down, gazing up with its uncomplaining face, responsible and hopeless and infinitely sad, and Ruth was filled with guilt.

She woke sweating and horrified, convinced that she had unwittingly done something cruel. Arthur Barton had loved his wife. Perhaps he had always hoped she would come to love him in return. Even after death, he had nursed a secret hope. But Elsie was with her sailor, and the curtains billowed inwards in the sudden wind . . . The dream was happening again and Ruth pulled herself away from it. The grey light of dawn came through her window and she stared at the pale rectangle with wide open eyes. Gradually the dream faded, but she lay awake for a long time, dozing off again when sunshine began to warm the bedroom.

Ruth was almost inclined not to go out with her mother on the Meals on Wheels round that day, but the thought of the sociology project nagged. And besides, she reflected, the best way to dispel a bad dream was to replace it with reality. The thought of the little brown, suffering creature, which followed at her heels in a forlorn hope of being loved, haunted her waking life.

At the depot the supervisor, Mrs Charlesworth, was checking items on a clipboard. She wore a hat and a tweed dress with a string of pearls, topped by a large white apron. She looked up as Ruth and her mother came in and said, 'One less on your round today, Mrs Astey. Poor old Elsie Barton was found dead this morning. The milkman knocked for his money and when she didn't answer he raised the alarm. Awfully sensible chap. He knew she hadn't been out of that flat for years. Neighbours used to get all her shopping.'

Ruth felt herself turn cold. Perhaps that was why Mrs Barton had given her the photograph. 'You must tell him,' she had said. 'I think I may not be able to.' Ruth thought of the purple face and the wheezing breath. The old woman must have known she was going to die. She was with her sailor, long-drowned after all, and so the man-dog had no owner.

'Now, don't you go getting upset,' said Mrs Astey, glancing at Ruth's white face. 'I know it's a bit of a shock, but really when you think of it, she's best out of it all, poor old dear. She was very vague in her mind. It wasn't much of a life for her.' She turned to Mrs Charlesworth and added, 'Are the Council clearing the flat?'

'Oh, yes, straight away,' said Mrs Charlesworth. 'There's such a waiting list, you see, and she had no relatives.'

'Everything does somebody some good,' said Ruth's mother. Then she added: 'Well, we'd better get loaded up.' Outside, she turned to Ruth and said kindly: 'Look, love, if you feel a bit yukky about Mrs Barton, I'll drop you home. You don't have to come if you don't want to.'

'It's all right,' said Ruth. 'Honestly.' She had a strong feeling of unfinished business. There was something purposeful about the man-dog, still close at her heels.

In the car her mother said, 'How's your project coming along? You're certainly getting lots of material for it!'

'The trouble is,' Ruth said sombrely, 'most of the material isn't really sociology.' And they drove on in silence.

Mrs Astey pulled up outside the block of flats where Mrs

Barton had lived. 'Mrs Mills on the ground floor,' she said, 'and Mr Cartwright on the fifth.'

'I'll do Mrs Mills,' said Ruth. Morbidly, she wondered how they had brought Mrs Barton's body down from her flat if the lift was still out of order. She was such a fat woman. As if in answer, her mother pressed the green button and said: 'Good, it's working today.' The aluminium door slid aside then closed again when Mrs Astey had got in.

Ruth took packets of shepherd's pie and rice pudding from the boot of the car and carried them across to Mrs Mills' door. She handed them in to the round-faced little woman, took the money and went back to the car. It was like the dream, with the concrete steps leading upwards and the man-dog quietly at her heels, undemanding and sad.

Ruth stared into the boot of the car, still hoping she had dropped the seaside photograph in there yesterday when she had reached in for meal packages. But there was no sign of it anywhere on the carpeted floor of the boot. Ruth felt that she had betrayed the old woman's trust. Although there had never been any hope of locating Billy, she ought not to have lost the photograph – not so soon and so carelessly. It was a heartless thing to have done, specially now that the old woman was dead.

The lift door slid aside and Ruth turned, expecting to see her mother. Instead, two Council workmen in orange boiler suits came out pushing a large porter's trolley between them. It was piled high with furniture and tied-up bundles of old newspapers and books and bedding, topped by several black plastic dustbin bags tied at the neck. A dust cart, Ruth realised, was standing a little distance from her mother's car. As the men passed her with the trolley one of the black plastic bags keeled sideways and fell onto the pavement, bursting open. Old stockings and half-eaten packets of biscuits spilled out and, sliding over the top of them to land at Ruth's feet came the framed photograph of Arthur Barton. It stared up with its well-brushed hair, its face honest and dog-like and sad. Ruth's blood ran cold. As the men began to shuffle the stuff into a new bag she bent and picked the photograph up

'Friend of yours, is he?' asked one of the men, grinning.

'Not exactly,' said Ruth. She tucked the photograph into the car's stretchy pocket inside the door, where nobody could see it.

'I'd better do Miss Beresford,' said Ruth's mother when they reached the next stop. 'She asked me to get her some stamps and she's frightfully deaf. You'd have an awful job explaining.'

'I'll do Mr Jacks, then,' said Ruth with some relief. Mr Jacks was splendidly normal. She took the two packs out of the car and went up the front path, half expecting him to open the door at her approach as he had done the previous day. He did not, so she rang the bell and heard it peal loudly in the hall. Of course, she was quite a lot earlier today. After a few minutes she rang again. The stillness of the house was suddenly alarming. She retreated a few paces from the step and saw that the dining-room window was open. The curtains fluttered inwards in the summer breeze. Ruth walked carefully across the lawn and looked in through the window.

The table had been used for an elaborate meal. An empty champagne bottle stood in a bucket of melted ice and a multi-branched silver candlestick held the burned-down stumps of red candles. Two people had eaten at the table, for the crumpled napkins had been thrown onto the starched cloth beside two coffee cups, and two small glasses were sticky with the remains of Benedictine. But Mr Jacks sat alone at the table now, his hand extended as if he grasped another hand. He smiled as he gazed into another face and, on the white tablecloth between him and his unseen friend, lay the dog-eared seaside photograph.

'Mr Jacks,' whispered Ruth. But even as she heard her

own voice she knew that his eyes stared at nothing at all and the smile on his face was still and cold. Mr Jacks was dead.

'What I don't understand,' said Ruth's mother over a cup of tea later on, 'is how that photograph got there. Are you *sure* you didn't give it to him, Ruth?'

'Of course I didn't,' said Ruth. 'It was in my cardigan pocket. I suppose I must have dropped it. There was a gust of wind when I opened the front door.'

'It's such an extraordinary way to die,' said her mother. 'Sitting over that celebration dinner. What on earth was he celebrating? Some kind of reunion?'

'Perhaps,' said Ruth. She dropped her hand to touch the man-dog's fur. She had smuggled the framed photograph of Arthur Barton upstairs where it now lay hidden in the drawer of her bedside table.

'One mustn't get involved, of course,' said Mrs Astey, 'but I can't help wondering whom he had dinner with. It seems so odd for anyone to leave him sitting at the table like that.'

The man-dog glanced up at Ruth gravely and she wrinkled her nose at him. In a way, it was rather nice having someone about who demanded no explanations. Poor Arthur. He could never have demanded anything. All he wanted was someone to love. His shaggy fur looked glossier today.

'It must have been some old friend,' persisted Ruth's mother. 'Could have been an old ship-mate, perhaps. It seems he was a sea-faring man. The police will soon find out who it was – they've got the whole thing in hand.'

Ruth glanced down again, and gave a little laugh.

'I don't see what's funny about that,' said her mother.

'No – nothing,' said Ruth hastily. She would have to be careful. It had been silly of her to laugh. But it was the first time she had seen Arthur smile.

FIVE

The Fen Tiger

The removal van lurched away down the rutted drive, empty. Matthew Bennett stared after it, regretting the departure of the cheerful men with their green baize aprons and their transistor radio. He looked back into the kitchen where his mother was fishing newspaper-wrapped objects out of a tea-chest.

'Shall I let Sandy out?' asked Matthew, for yowls of protest were coming from the cat basket.

'I should shut the door first,' said his mother, unwrapping a vase and looking round for somewhere to put it. But Matthew had already opened the basket and the cat streaked through his hands and out of the open door.

'Oh, no!' cried Matthew. 'He'll get lost!'

Jean Bennett tried to sound reassuring. 'He won't have gone far,' she said, then raised her voice as Matthew went out. 'Keep away from the buildings! They're so derelict, you might fall through the floor or something.'

'I'll be all right,' Matthew called back. After all, he was nearly eight. Ignoring the farm buildings, which in any case stood too far from the house for Sandy to have reached them, Matthew pushed open the rotting gate which led into a kind of jungle. Ivy-burdened apple trees rose from thickets of blackberry and the nettles were as tall as Matthew himself, standing like an army of lancers with their mindless, white-flowered heads reared above the cohorts of stinging leaves.

Cautiously, Matthew made his way through the jungle until he was stopped by rusted strands of barbed wire across a gap in the hedge. Water glinted on the far side of it and

Matthew pushed aside some elder branches with their bunches of green-black berries to look more closely. If it was a stream, he thought, it would be a good place to come and play. Better than the house with its musty smell and broken windows.

It was a stream, quite a narrow one running at the bottom of a deep ditch. And a man stood on the opposite bank, swaying slightly as if he found it hard to keep his balance. He was staring at the house with fixed intensity.

The September sun was low in the sky and Matthew put his hand up to shade his eyes as he squinted at the man's dark bulk. Behind him, the flat fields stretched to a horizon as straight as if it had been drawn with a ruler.

'Hello,' said Matthew.

The man did not reply. His face was as rutted and immobile as the surface of the farm drive but his red-rimmed eyes flicked momentarily as he glanced at Matthew and away again to go on staring at the house. They were strange eyes, Matthew thought, such a light brown as to seem almost orange in the dark, weather-beaten face. The lids were sagging and inflamed. The man's clothes were too old to have any discernible colour, the jacket and trousers and cap moulded by long wear to be part of their owner's shape. But he had a yellow scarf tied round his neck, a bright stripe against his darkness.

Matthew found the scarf easier to talk to than the man's face. 'Er – do you want to see Mummy?' he asked it. 'Shall I fetch her?'

The man laughed shortly, showing broken teeth. 'No,' he said. 'What would I want to see her for?' He lurched a little then recovered his balance.

'Or Daddy,' said Matthew. 'He's upstairs doing something to the water. It doesn't work.'

'That won't,' said the man. 'Nothing here will work for you, boy.' The orange eyes glanced briefly at Matthew, showing their red corners, then resumed their hungry stare at the house. 'If I couldn't work it,' the man said, 'nobody can.'

Matthew didn't understand why his parents had come to this place. It had been all right in London. 'What do you mean?' he asked rather crossly because he suddenly wished he was back in his little room at home.

'That broke me,' said the man. 'I'd never have sold it else. People who bought it couldn't work it. The place wouldn't have them. Nor it won't have you, boy.' He laughed again and yet, Matthew thought, he seemed angry at the same time, rather like Sandy on a hot day, when he lay purring in the sun but with the tip of his tail twitching. If you touched him then, he might ball himself suddenly round your hand, clutching and kicking and biting.

'I must go and find my cat,' said Matthew, remembering. 'We let him out of his basket and he rushed off.'

'He won't last long,' said the man with grim satisfaction. He dragged his gaze away from the house and turned to lurch off along the dyke. He looked back and shouted: 'None of you will last long!'

Matthew gave a little shiver. The sun had touched the horizon, its lower edge seeming to bulge out as if the ball of fire was collapsing into the landscape instead of slipping down behind it.

Sandy was in a shed near the back door, crouched under some scrap timber which leaned against the wall. The floor was covered with coal dust and Matthew was very dirty by the time he had managed to gather up the frightened cat.

'Oh, *Matthew*!' said his mother as he carried Sandy into the kitchen. 'Did you *have* to get into such a mess?'

'I didn't mean to,' said Matthew. 'I had to move some wood.' His father was sitting on the edge of the kitchen table, drinking a mug of tea. He looked even dirtier than Matthew.

'Well, never mind,' said Jean Bennett, 'but you'll have to go to bed unbathed.'

'I'll get it right tomorrow,' said Matthew's father. 'It

wants a new ballcock in the tank.'

Matthew took his mug of milky tea. 'Have you found my Ted yet?' he enquired casually. Sandy was creeping round the edges of the kitchen with his ears back, looking for a way out.

'For goodness' sake, Matthew,' his mother exploded, 'can't you manage without Ted for just one night? You're a big boy now.'

'I know,' said Matthew. He didn't want to make a fuss. But the room upstairs had high ceilings with black beams across them, and the wallpaper bulged away from the walls, piebald with damp, and the window was broken. And it smelt funny.

'Better feed that cat, then he'll settle down,' said Peter Bennett.

'Oh, all right,' said his wife tiredly. She brushed a strand of hair back from her forehead with her wrist and added, 'The cat food's in one of those boxes. I don't know which.'

'I'll look for it,' said Matthew. As he started to delve, he saw his father get off the table and put his arm round Matthew's mother. 'No regrets, love?' he asked her. 'We knew it would be tough at first, didn't we? But it's better than sitting in Fulham, frittering away the redundancy money.'

' 'Course it is,' said Jean loyally.

'I found the cat food,' said Matthew, holding up the tin. 'Now can we look for my Ted?'

The next morning, Matthew discovered that the wallpaper was delightfully easy to pull of the wall. Ted lounged on the bed with his usual limpness because his stuffing had left his middle and gone to the ends of his fat paws. He watched what Matthew was doing through his single remaining black and orange glass eye. Matthew felt much better this morning. The wallpaper came off in huge pieces, layers of it all stuck together, tearing away in long strips that ran right up to the ceiling. Sometimes the plaster came off as well, and fell on the floorboards with rattling thumps.

Matthew's mother came in and Matthew looked round a little guiltily. Perhaps he should have asked before he started on the wallpaper. But his mother had a funny expression on her face, with a little quiver at the corner of her mouth. Matthew knew it was nothing to do with the wallpaper.

'Darling,' said Jean, 'I'm afraid something very sad has happened. Sandy's been run over. Daddy found him right down at the end of the drive, on the main road. He can't have known anything about it,' she added.

Matthew went slowly across to the bed. A great ache was rising in his throat. 'He didn't like it here,' he said, picking Ted up by one paw. And then he was weeping into the patchy orange fur fabric between Ted's ears, thinking of Sandy's glossy orange coat, dead and gone and never to be stroked again.

'I expect he got out through a broken window, you see,' said his mother wretchedly. 'But we'll get another kitten, Matthew.' She came and sat beside him and hugged him to her. 'And we might have a dog now we're in the country. And Daddy's going to get a goat to help clear up all the weeds, and some chickens and maybe some ducks. There's lots to look forward to.'

Matthew nodded dutifully. But the words of the man who stood at the edge of the dyke rang in his ears. 'He won't last long. None of you will last long.' A small, obstinate determination began to grow at the back of Matthew's mind. The man had been right about Sandy. But that was enough. Matthew wiped his eyes with Ted's paw. 'A dog would be nice,' he said shakily.

When Peter Bennett came back from the town at lunchtime with a new ballcock for the hot water tank he said, 'I went into the local for a pint. Found out quite a lot about this place. Seems it used to belong to an old boy called Calvin Jarrett – a real old Fen tiger. But he went bankrupt. They say he took to the bottle and drank all his money away. Anyhow, he had to sell up for what he could get. The blokes in the pub said he put a curse on the place and that's why the Kings couldn't make a go of it and sold it to us.'

'I never heard such rubbish,' said Matthew's mother. 'Curse, indeed!'

'What's a Fen tiger?' asked Matthew.

'That's the name for the old Fenland farmers,' his father explained. 'Living out here in this wild, flat country, they reckoned you had to have the spirit of a tiger to make a go of it.' He smiled at his wife. 'I reckon they breed pretty good tigers in Fulham, too.'

'You bet,' she said stoutly.

Matthew was not listening. He could see the orange eyes in the dark face, the scarf like a yellow stripe across the heavy shoulders. The jagged teeth were bared again as the man gave his short laugh. 'None of you will last'. Deep in his pockets, Matthew clenched his fists.

Matthew started school the following week, walking down the drive each morning to wait for the bus in the flat, windswept landscape. He had always thought the earth was brown, but here in the Fens it was purple-black. Water ran sparkling in the dykes which criss-crossed the fields and the clouds scudded so fast across the sky that everything seemed to be moving; pylons, fields, chicken wire, grass and the road where Matthew stood.

Coming home from school on the bus a few days later, the boy who sat next to Matthew said, 'Hear about old Jarrett? Him that put the curse on your place?'

'That's silly,' said Matthew crossly. 'People can't put curses on things.' You won't last long, the man had said.

'Don't know about that,' said the boy. 'But he won't do no more cursing. He's dead. Killed himself.'

Matthew stared at him. The man's dark face was clear in his mind. What would he look like now that he was dead? He thought of television thrillers. A round, red hole in the forehead? A shirt covered in blood?'

'They found him hanging in the shed behind his cottage,' said the boy, who had sticking-out ears. 'He tied a meat-hook to a beam in the roof and hooked it through that yellow scarf he used to wear. Standing on a box. Then he kicked the box away. They say his face was black.'

Matthew suddenly felt sick. He was glad the bus was slowing down as it approached the drive to the Bennetts' smallholding. He got up and made his way down the gangway. Nobody else got off here.

Matthew walked up the rutted drive and thought about death. The wind ruffled the surface of the puddles which lay in the ruts and the sky was reflected in them. Sandy had been alive and then he was just a squashed, messy thing. But where had Sandy gone, the real Sandy with his ideas about birds which made him lash his tail, and his purring comfort on Matt's knee after he had been fed? And where was the man who had stood on the edge of the dyke?

The drive was bordered by a thin, overgrown hedge whose bare branches did little to keep off the cutting wind. Matthew pulled the hood of his anorak over his head and fished with a mitted hand for the laces to pull it tight. And then he saw the tiger.

The pattern of branching black stripes seemed like a part of the hedge at first, a section of the parade which flicked like an irregular railing past the dying sun. But as Matthew walked, a part of the hedge walked with him on huge, silent paws. It turned its head to look at him with orange eyes, red at the corners, and its bulk was dark against the sky. The heavy-chinned mouth was open a little as the animal muttered to itself in a purr or a snarl, and the smell of it was carried on the wind to Matthew, musky and intimate. He stood still, the hair on his scalp crawling with terror – and the tiger had gone.

Matthew stood motionless for several long seconds, staring at the black branches of the hedge as they moved in the wind. Then he ran, splashing recklessly through the puddles until he reached the kitchen door.

'Good gracious me!' said his mother. 'You look as if you'd seen a ghost!'

'I thought I'd seen a tiger,' admitted Matthew. It sounded silly, and his mother laughed. 'If anyone had lost a tiger we'd have heard about it,' she said. 'And how!'

The death of Calvin Jarrett was reported in the local paper. The paragraph was headed: 'Suicide of Retired Farmer' and spoke of his growing depression in recent years. Peter Bennett read it with interest. 'This place used to have five hundred acres!' he said. 'Says here it was sold off bit by bit. To pay for the old man's booze, I suppose. What a way to go.'

' "And when they get to feeling old",' Jean quoted, ' "They up and shoot themselves, I'm told." '

Matthew stared at her. How could she be so light-hearted about it? Death was horribly real here. That very morning, his father had found a trail of feathers leading from the half-derelict shed where he had installed some Golden Comet chickens. Matthew had gone with him, to find a hen's foot by the field gate, another just beyond it, and then a contemptuous scattering of wings, head and a host of feathers which indicated that the fox had sat down to eat his dinner at leisure. And Matthew had seen the tiger again, lying along an apple branch in the weed-choked orchard, the tip of its tail dangling among the brambles and twitching in a restless, menacing way. The tiger had looked at him with its orange eyes and Matthew knew what it meant. You won't last long.

The Bennetts were finding the smallholding hard going. The buildings revealed layer upon layer of rottenness. Doors could not be replaced upon their jambs because the timbers hung loosely in crumbling stonework which fell away in clouds of rubbly dust. Water lay close under the earth's surface and seeped into the house during wet weather, crawling up the walls to push off the new paint like a sloughed skin. It seemed that nothing would make the buildings fox-proof and the stock of chickens dwindled nightly. The few remaining birds took refuge on the high beams of the barn and as October advanced they began to moult and laid no more eggs. Peter Bennett bought a goat and tethered her in the orchard jungle, where she managed to twine her rope tightly round an apple tree and was found strangled a few hours later.

The tiger sat among the wild sunflowers under the elder bush with its clusters of black berries, and smiled. The yellow stripe flowed up its chest and across its heavy shoulders and its musky smell was in Matthew's nostrils. He felt very alone and very afraid.

That afternoon it began to rain heavily and Matthew's mother, running across the yard to snatch in the washing from the line, slipped on the muddy flagstones and crashed down across the boot-scraper outside the kitchen door, breaking her leg like a matchstick.

'That's all we needed,' said Peter Bennett when they all came back from the hospital. He fetched a stool to put under his wife's plastered leg, then filled the kettle. 'Straight to bed after tea, Matthew.' he said. 'It's very late after all that hanging about in Casualty.'

Matthew did not argue. He had other things to think about.

'What a thing to happen,' Jean lamented, staring at the white plaster as if it belonged to some unwelcome stranger. 'Just when we'd started this drainage project and everything.'

'Never mind, love,' said her husband, throwing a couple of tea bags into the pot. 'We'll pull through. The land's good – look at the crops everyone else round here has got. If we can just get it cleared and drained, and throw off this unlucky streak, we'll be fine.'

'I'll go to bed now,' said Matthew as soon as he had

finished his tea.

'Good lad,' said his father. 'I'll come and see you when I've washed the tea things.'

Upstairs, it was almost dark and rain pattered on the window, but Matthew did not switch on the light. He crossed the room and collected Ted from where he lay sprawled on the pillow then went over to the window, rubbing his upper lip with Ted's paw as he used to when he was small.

The tiger was close tonight. It paced to and fro in the rain, just beyond the roughly-mown piece of grass outside the sitting-room which Matthew's mother called 'the lawn'. Among the withered stalks of cow-parsley the tiger crossed and re-crossed the bars of light which shone from the downstairs windows. Its wet coat gleamed as though it was black all over but when the tiger raised its head to stare up at Matthew the yellow stripe on its chest was as livid as a scar. Even from behind the glass, Matthew could smell the musky, choking scent. He opened the window and leaned out. 'What do you want?' he asked, staring into the angry orange eyes. The tiger stared back silently.

Matthew had never managed to speak to the tiger before. Its appearance had always so paralysed him with fear that he had stood motionless, praying for it to go away. But, hugging Ted's comforting woolliness in the safety of his upstairs room, he felt braver.

'You've got to leave us alone,' he said more loudly. But his own unanswered question echoed in his ears. The tiger wanted something. It would not go away unappeased. A sacrifice, Matthew thought. He stared into the orange eyes out there in the falling rain and remembered the awful Bible story Miss Leggitt had told them at school, about the man who had been willing to sacrifice his own son to give God what He demanded.

Matthew shut his eyes for a moment and buried his face in Ted's threadbare fur. He wished he was grown-up, like the man in the Bible, then perhaps it would seem easier. When he looked again, the tiger had gone.

It was dark when Matthew woke and he wondered in a confused way why the room had seemed to be shining red through his closed eyelids. A crackle of thunder came in explanation, building to a series of bangs which decayed reluctantly into a dying rumble. Matthew shrank under the blankets. Rain was rattling on the window like handfuls of stones.

Suddenly the room was full of the smell of the tiger, thick and foul and urgent. 'Please God,' Matthew prayed silently from under the bedclothes, 'make it go away.' But there was only one word in answer to Matthew's prayer, and he did not know whether it came from God or the tiger. Sacrifice, it said. Sacrifice.

Matthew got out of bed. He wiped the misty window with his pyjama sleeve and looked out. At first he could not see the tiger but its smell was pouring in through his mouth and nose and he knew it was closer than it had ever been. He opened the window and looked down with the rain lashing his face and chest. Then he gasped. The tiger was standing on its hind legs with his huge front feet almost reaching Matthew's window-sill. Its talons were dug deeply into the pink-washed stucco and as its eyes met Matthew's it subsided slowly onto its hind quarters with its front legs still extended, the claws raking down the wall and leaving deep vertical gouges. It sat like that for a moment, with its paws on the wall and its orange eyes still fixed on Matthew's face while the rain streamed over its striped coat. Then it turned in a single lithe movement and made off towards the kitchen door, glancing back for a last look at Matthew as it went.

Lightning threaded the sky like the dazzling roots of some unimaginable plant and the Fens were suddenly visible in the dancing blue light. Then there was blackness. Matthew pulled the window shut. His pyjama jacket was soaked. The clap of thunder began with a tearing noise as though the sky was being ripped apart.

Ted was still between the sheets. His fur felt very warm when Matthew picked him up. He opened the door of his room and crept downstairs. He took his anorak from the peg behind the kitchen door and put it on, tucking Ted inside it, then pushed his feet into his Wellington boots. He slid back the bolt on the kitchen door and stepped out into the rain.

The smell of the tiger was choking, its purring, snarling, vibrating presence as close as Matthew's own heartbeats. He took Ted from under his anorak and held him out, blinded by the lashing rain. 'You can have him!' he shouted. 'He's all I've got. My best thing. Like the man in the Bible.'

Then the tiger was there, and the dark centres of its orange eyes glowed blood-red. A small part of Matthew's panic-stricken mind was grieved that Ted was getting wet. 'Take him!' he shouted desperately. 'And then you must leave us alone!'

The tiger gathered itself slowly, the muscles tightening under its striped coat. Then it sprang. And in that instant, with the tiger's bulk black above him in the lightning-torn sky, Matthew realised his mistake. It wasn't only Ted the tiger wanted. It was him.

Upstairs, Jean Bennett had nudged her husband uneasily. 'Peter,' she said, 'do wake up. I think Matthew's out of bed. I'm sure I heard the stairs creak, but it's difficult to know with this storm.'

'M'm,' agreed Peter, not opening his eyes.

'You know he's walked in his sleep sometimes,' Jean went on. After an unresponsive pause she began to get out of bed but Peter sat up and said: 'Don't be daft. You can't be clodding about with your leg in plaster.' He pulled on his dressing-gown a little irritably and Jean said, 'Listen! Wasn't that Matthew calling out?'

'Don't think so,' said Peter. He opened the bedroom door – and then the screaming began.

By the time the doctor left, it was getting light. He dropped his stethoscope into his bag and snapped it shut. 'He's very deeply shocked,' he said. 'I've given him a sedative but you will need to keep a careful eye on him.' He paused at the door, frowning. 'It's the lacerations I can't understand,' he added. 'You found him lying face down in the yard, you said – so if he'd been sleep-walking he could have tripped and fallen. That would explain the bruising and shock. But the lacerations on both sides of the back, right through a quilted anorak –' He shook his head again. 'It's as though someone was trying to pick the boy up with a giant pair of tongs.'

'He was perfectly all right when he went to bed,' said Jean for the tenth time. 'I just can't understand it.'

'I'll be back after morning surgery,' said the doctor. He glanced at Jean Bennett's plastered leg and added: 'You've been having a bad time lately, haven't you?'

'You can say that again,' said Peter with feeling.

'Perhaps your luck will change from now on,' said the doctor, and went out to his car in the dawn light. The storm had blown itself out.

Matthew's injuries healed and after a time he allowed himself to be dressed and brought downstairs, but his eyes gazed endlessly at something his parents could not see, and he did not speak. In mounting alarm and then despair they took him to one specialist after another and, on the advice of one of them, bought a puppy in place of the vanished Ted. Matthew seemed to like the softness of the puppy's fur when they held it to his face, and once he tried to rub his upper lip with its paw. But the puppy whined and struggled away, and Matthew cried a little. But he said nothing.

The doctor's words proved to be prophetic and the smallholding entered a period of easy success. The drainage scheme resulted in a dry and much warmer house and the black fields began to crop well. With patience and some expert local help, the buildings were restored to a usable condition and the livestock flourished. Despite their grief over the silent, white-faced boy who watched the hedges and the long grass in a kind of uncanny stillness, the Bennetts could not help enjoying their prosperity. In time, they were able to buy a parcel of adjoining land.

One late afternoon, Peter Bennett set off along the far side of the dyke to pace his newly-acquired acres. He paused at the gap in the orchard hedge, thinking that he must take down those strands of rusty barbed wire. Perhaps he would put some railway sleepers down as a bridge over the dyke. The red sun was low in the sky behind him as he gazed with the pride of ownership at the house whose pink walls gleamed between the branches of the apple trees. Some deep scratches in the plaster under Matthew's bedroom window showed up clearly in the slanting light and Peter made a note that he must patch them next time he had some cement mixed. But all these jobs took time, and it had been a busy year.

Peter turned away to continue his tour of inspection. Then something glinting at his feet caught his attention. He stopped and picked the object up. It was a small glass eye, black-centred and orange-rimmed, with a piece of thick wire attached to the back of it. The eye, though slightly muddy, gazed up from the palm of Peter's hand with vacuous good temper, and Peter's blood ran cold. He had seen that amiable half-blind gaze for too many years not to recognise it now. He put the eye in his pocket and went home, beckoning from the kitchen door to his wife, who sat feeding the big, heavy-limbed boy with a teaspoon.

After a muttered conference, they agreed that the sight of Ted's eye might upset Matthew, so they threw it in the bin. And Matthew, opening his mouth obediently for the warm stuff they were putting into it, gazed into the huge orange eyes which were his whole world, and was surrounded by noisy, smelly purring.

Jean Bennett gazed at her son doubtfully as she wiped a dribble of food from his chin. 'Sometimes,' she said, 'he looks as if he's smiling.'

SIX

Dundee Cake

The kitchen was full of the smell of baking, warm and steamy, clouding the windows against the November afternoon. Robin's mother cracked two eggs into a bowl and beat them briskly with a fork. Then she said: 'Be a dear and pop down to Granny's on your bike – see if there's anything she wants.'

Robin had been expecting this. Nowadays there always seemed to be some good reason why his mother hadn't time to go and see Granny herself. 'Do I *have* to?' he complained.

His mother squinted at the figures on the scale as she tipped flour onto its pan. 'I was going to make cherry buns for your tea,' she said, 'but if I have to go down to Granny's myself –'

Robin knew when he was beaten. He got up reluctantly.

'She gets lonely,' his mother went on apologetically. 'I mean, she doesn't see many people.'

'She sees people who aren't there,' said Robin darkly.

'She wanders in her mind a bit,' his mother agreed. 'Lots of old people do.'

'Wanders!' Robin was aggrieved. 'Last time I was there she'd got the table set for all her family. Auntie Alice and Auntie Edie and Uncle Jack and I don't know who. She even introduced me to them all and I had to pretend to shake hands. And who's this Callum she's always on about?'

His mother paused fractionally in her stirring in of the flour. 'Someone she used to know,' she said, and went on stirring.

'You mean, a boy friend?' asked Robin, intrigued. 'Gosh!

Didn't your father mind?'

'It was nothing like that,' said his mother primly. 'I never heard any mention of anyone called Callum when I was a child. I think he must have been her first sweetheart – someone she knew before she was married. It's all those early things she talks about these days.'

'You're telling me,' said Robin with feeling.

His mother wiped her hands on her apron and said: 'You can take her a round of shortbread. She'll like that.'

'Yes, she's keen on all those Scottish things,' said Robin, getting his anorak from the peg behind the door. 'She seems to have forgotten she lives in England now. She always calls me Hamish.'

'That was her brother.' Robin's mother slipped the fresh-baked round of shortbread into a brown paper bag and folded the loose edge underneath. 'Now, take care of this,' she instructed. 'Put it flat in your saddle bag so it doesn't break. They don't look half as nice once they're broken.'

'All right,' said Robin. He took the flat package carefully in both hands and stood back for his mother to open the back door. As he passed her she bent down and gave him a kiss. 'Thanks for going,' she said. 'I'll do it tomorrow – promise.'

'It's okay,' said Robin stoically.

He put the shortbread carefully into his saddle bag and switched on his front and rear lamps. It was almost dark and drizzling a little. Still, it wasn't far to Granny's.

When his grandmother opened the door, disappointment clouded her face as it always did. 'Ah, Hamish,' she said, looking past him to see if anyone else stood in the darkness. 'It's you.'

Robin did not bother to try and correct the name. 'I brought you some shortbread,' he said. 'Mum just made it.'

'Come away in, dear.' The old lady turned from the door, leaving Robin to shut it, and prodded her way, stick first, across the carpet to the fire. Robin saw with foreboding that the table was laid with the best china, the place settings crowded onto the lace cloth and the old-fashioned, three-tiered cake stand set proudly in the centre although it was empty of cakes. There was never any food at Granny's strange little tea parties. Robin supposed that imaginary people ate imaginary things. It seemed logical. He took the round of shortbread out of its brown paper bag, beautifully intact, and slid it carefully onto the top tier of the cake stand.

'Shortbread,' said his grandmother in tones of interested surprise. 'Goodness.' She reached forward and touched the fluted edge of the shortbread with her fingers as if to assure herself that it was real. Then she glanced at some invisible person beside her and smiled. 'Isn't that nice, Alice?' she said conversationally. 'Hamish has brought us some shortbread.'

Robin shifted uneasily. 'Yes, well,' he said, 'is there anything you want me to do, Granny? Have you got enough coal in?'

'There's plenty of people can be getting the coal,' said his grandmother. Then she brightened. 'Callum will do it when he comes. Did I tell you, Hamish? Callum is coming for me tonight. He is coming back from India, after all these years!'

Robin looked at the pale blue eyes which smiled so delightedly, and at the short, tufty white hair. Bits of it always seemed to stick up in the wrong direction. 'That's nice for you,' he said kindly, but his grandmother's gaze had darted away in a new direction.'Did you hear that, Edie? Callum will be here tonight.' Then she laughed with a trace of malice. 'I do believe you fancied him yourself at one time, dear, did you not? But I've always known he'd come back for me one day.'

Robin looked in the coal scuttle, which was almost empty. He piled the last lumps onto the fire and took the scuttle out to the shed to fill it. When he came back, his grandmother was sitting in her chair, frowning at the table in a dissatisfied way. 'Look,' she said briskly, turning to Robin, 'that short-bread is not going to be enough. We need a cake.'

Robin's heart sank. A few months ago she had insisted on buying a large haggis and Robin's family had fetched up eating the beastly thing fried for breakfast. Robin's father had given his share to the cat, which was afterwards sick on the lawn.

'I'll ask Mum if she can make you a cake,' Robin said cautiously. Given time, the old lady would probably forget the idea. But she was scrabbling urgently in her purse. 'No, no,' she said. 'Callum will want a Dundee cake. He always said tea was not tea without a Dundee cake. And there's no time to make one – he'll be here very soon. We'll need to buy one.' She held out a pound note to Robin.

'But you'll have such a job finishing it all on your own,' he protested uneasily. 'And I think they're quite expensive.' He was not at all sure that a pound would be enough.

The blue eyes froze. 'You will not tell me how to manage my own affairs, Hamish,' she snapped. 'Just go along to Tarbert's when I tell you. They have quite good cakes there. And quickly, now.' As Robin shrugged and accepted the money she turned to her invisible audience. 'Always such an obstinate boy,' she told them. 'Do you mind the day he would not wear his Sunday kilt, Alice? Said he had lost it, if you please. The whole house upside down looking for it before we could be away to the kirk.' Her attention was back on Robin. 'Now, you tell them at Tarbert's I want a good Dundee cake, mind! The best they have for Callum McBride's return.'

Robin pushed the pound note into his anorak pocket and went out to his bike. He could hear the rise and fall of his grandmother's voice in the empty room as she conversed with Alice and Edie and whoever else it was. He rode off into the rain, glad that the baker's was in the parade of shops just round the corner. It was called Bloomfield's, of course, not Tarbert's – but he had given up expecting anything his grandmother said to be right.

It was quite dark now, and the lights of the shops were

reflected in the wet road as he approached the parade. It was raining heavily. Ahead of him, Robin saw a car pulling away from the kerb just outside the baker's. Good, he thought. That's handy. As he was coasting into the space he was aware of a car alongside him, very close, making for the same space. Had the driver not seen Robin's rear light? He felt a moment's wild alarm.

'You'll be Isobel Wishart's wee brother,' said the baker, looking at Robin over the tops of his glasses. The Scottish accent irritated Robin, who was shaken by his near-miss with the car outside the shop. Did *everyone* have to be Scottish around here? And what did the man mean, anyway? His grandmother's name was Isobel, but she was Mrs Campbell.

'I want a Dundee cake,' he said rather crossly, then added, 'please.'

'That'll be for Callum McBride,' said the baker, nodding sagely. 'Coming back for the lassie at last.'

Robin frowned. It seemed odd that the man should know about all that. The baker selected a round, rich cake, its top thickly studded with almonds and its fat sides encased in a tartan ribbon. 'How about that, now?' he said with pride. 'Two and nine.' Robin nodded, not understanding what he meant, and the man put the cake into a white cardboard box. He folded the lid down and tucked it in, then tied the box with white string from a reel mounted on the side of a wooden display cabinet. Across the top of the box in flowing letters was inscribed the legend, 'F. Tarbert – Bakers and Confectioners.' Robin stared at it, puzzled, then decided that Bloomfield's must be using up old stock. He gave the man a pound note and, still thinking about the name on the box, pushed what seemed a large amount of change into his pocket and left the shop.

Robin stared in amazement at the lit windows of his grandmother's house as he cycled up the drive. Shadows moved across the glowing curtains and somebody was playing the piano. What on earth was going on? Surely he had not come to the wrong house? He stopped and looked up at the arch over the front door where the name of the house was incised into the stone. 'Braemar'. No, that was it. He rang the bell.

The door was flung open at once. 'Here's Hamish with the cake!' his grandmother called, laughing. Robin stared at her. Suddenly, she was so pretty. Her hair was dark, a great mass of it braided and piled on top of her head. Had somebody given her a wig? And she seemed taller and slimmer, wearing a white silk dress and little shoes with pointed toes. He blinked and shook his head. Something had gone wrong. He must be dreaming. And yet this *was* his grandmother. Her voice was the same, and her essential being was unchanged. She put her arm round his shoulders to give him a quick, friendly hug. 'That's my good lad!' she said. As she took the cake from him she seemed to be bubbling with excitement. 'Any minute now!' she whispered, and glanced irresistibly at the door.

'I've got your change,' said Robin, fumbling in his anorak pocket. Again, he thought there seemed to be a surprisingly large number of coins.

'Och, just leave it on the hall table,' said his grandmother. 'Come away in.' she ran to the sitting-room door and called: 'Look, everyone! Hamish has brought the cake!'

As Robin put the money down he thought there was something wrong with it. The coins were the wrong size and shape, heavy and unfamiliar. But his grandmother took his hand and pulled him into the brightly-lit room, giving him no chance to examine the money more closely.

The people nodded and smiled when they saw him. There were big, solid men in hairy tweed jackets and women in silk dresses. They all wanted to shake hands or kiss him. Uncle Arthur, Auntie Louie, Auntie Alice, Cousin Jack . . . the woman who sat at the paino in a yellow dress with a deep vee at the back which showed her skinny shoulder blades looked up at him and smiled and he knew that she was Auntie Edie. Robin's head began to swim. Somehow, too, he was aware that it was beginning to hurt.

'Dundee cake!' the people were saying. 'Callum's favourite! He'll love you all the more, Isobel!'

Auntie Edie, finished playing, 'Will Ye No Come Back Again?' and said rather sadly: 'He always loved her.' And Robin's young grandmother stood with her face turned to stare across the room as if she could see beyond the curtained windows to whatever lay ouside in the rain and the darkness.

Robin suddenly began to feel frightened. 'You're not real!' he heard his own voice saying loudly. 'None of you are real!'

Somebody beside him took his shoulder in a big hand and squeezed it gently.

'Whisht now, laddie,' said Cousin Jack from the other side of the table. 'Listen!'

Silence had fallen in the room and the people stood stock-still like players in a game of Musical Statues, gestures arrested in mid-air and every head cocked attentively, listening. As faintly as a faraway voice came a single strand of music, wild and haunting and purposeful.

Bagpipes, thought Robin, and wondered at the shiver which prickled at the back of his neck. His grandmother ran into the hall and threw open the front door. Robin tried to follow her but his head was reeling and a darkness seemed to cloud his vision. He struggled to the sitting-room door and leaned against the jamb. Rain was blowing in through the open front door and the music of the pipes was close, strident now, and confident. And the white-clad figure of the girl who was his grandmother was out there in the darkness, wraith-like, running to meet the man who came striding towards her, kilt swinging, plaid flying in the night air.

Then all the people came rushing past Robin, shouting and laughing in welcome, bringing the tall man and the girl with rain-spattered hair in through the door. Callum McBride, with his pipes under his arm and his free hand round the slim shoulders of his sweetheart, laughed when he saw the table. 'Isobel,' he said. 'You even remembered the cake!'

It was not just cake, Robin saw. The table was groaning with cold meats and ham, mutton pies, bridies, apple turnovers, pancakes, scones, bannocks, oatcakes and black bun. It was all too much. The room was too hot and too bright. There were too many people, too close . . .

'It's not real!' Robin protested again in the fading moments of his consciousness. 'None of it is real!'

The friendly hand on his shoulder tightened its grip a little. 'It's all right, old boy,' somebody was saying. 'This is real, where you are now. Try and get your eyes open.'

Robin tried. Light poured in through the crack of vision he achieved. The hubbub of Scottish voices swam back again for a moment, then receded. He tried again to open his eyes. His head hurt. There was something blindingly white, very close to him. A white coat.

'Oh, Robin,' said a familiar, worried voice. 'Are you all right, love?'

'Mum!' said Robin, with the same kind of puzzled interest that his grandmother had expressed when she saw the shortbread. Then he fell asleep.

Next time he woke, everything seemed better. He was in a bed with a yellow cover on it, and there were flowered curtains all round, making a little room. His mother and father were both sitting by the bed, looking anxious, though they smiled when they saw that he was awake. The curtains parted and a man came in wearing a white coat. 'Ah,' he said, looking at Robin. 'Back in the land of the living, I see. You gave us a fright, young man.'

Robin wondered what he had done to give people a fright. He thought perhaps he should sit up and show an intelligent interest in this problem but a stab of pain shot through his head when he tried to move. Putting up a cautious hand, he found that his head was heavily bandaged.

'You don't want to move about too much,' advised the doctor. 'Not for a day or two. For someone who's been knocked off his bicycle you've had a lucky escape, but you'll want to take it easy for a bit.'

'I still can't think why he was down at the shops,' said Robin's mother fretfully. 'He didn't have any money in his pockets, so she can't have sent him to buy anything. Why didn't he come straight home?' She was looking at Robin's father as she said this and he shrugged as if she had asked him the question many times.

'Dundee cake,' said Robin.

Everyone stared. Robin's father said slowly: 'Now, that's a funny thing.' He leaned nearer to Robin, frowning over something he found difficult to understand. 'What do you mean, old chap? Did she send you for Dundee cake?'

'For Callum,' Robin explained. It seemed quite difficult to talk.

'Not too many questions,' said the doctor.

'No, of course not,' Robin's mother agreed. 'But I'd just sent her a round of shortbread, so I don't see why she thought she needed a Dundee cake. Sending the boy out . . .'

Robin found that he was terribly sleepy again. His mother's voice went echoing away.

It was some days later, when Robin was sitting up in bed assembling a plastic model kit of a Spitfire that his parents came and told him that his grandmother had died.

'Oh,' said Robin. He thought of his young grandmother running out into the darkness to meet Callum. Perhaps the young one and the old one couldn't exist at the same time. As long as they were happy, it didn't seem to matter much. He glanced up and realised that his mother and father were going to want to talk about it, so he screwed the cap back onto his tube of glue to stop it drying up. His parents watched him.

'The thing is,' said his father cautiously,' she was found dead the day you had your accident. And the police would quite like to know whether she was alive when you saw her. Not that we want to bother you,' he added hastily.

Robin's mother plunged into a torrent of words. 'When you didn't come back that evening, I mean, I'd been waiting tea for ages, I thought you'd probably got stuck at Granny's listening to one of her stories – you know how difficult it is to get away once she starts. I mean, how difficult it was –' She shook her head, biting her lip, then started again. 'Anyway, I got the car out and came down there, and she didn't answer the door. Well, I knew I hadn't seen you cycling back and I thought it was funny, so I let myself in. You know I always had a key just in case.'

Robin nodded. Nodding didn't hurt so much now.

'It was quite difficult to get the door open because she'd fallen just behind it,' his mother went on. 'It was a heart attack, the doctor says. And you weren't there. I was standing in the hall feeling frantic and I saw an ambulance go by with its light flashing, and I just knew it was you. Then a woman came by who'd seen the accident. She was very kind. Rang people up and –' She shook her head. 'It was all so awful.'

Robin fingered a wingtip experimentally. It seemed well stuck. He looked up. 'I am *sorry*, Mum,' he said. 'Upsetting you and everything. But I had to get the cake, you see. She wanted it for Callum.'

'So she was alive when you saw her?' asked his father.

'Oh, yes,' said Robin. 'And I bought the cake from Tarbert's –'

'Bloomfield's,' corrected his mother.

'Er – yes,' agreed Robin. 'And took it back to her house, and there were all these people there.' He frowned down at the Spitfire. He knew the next bit was going to sound silly.

'All what people?' asked his mother.

'Auntie Edie,' said Robin, 'and Uncle Arthur and Auntie Alice and all those people she'd been talking about.' He saw his parents glance at each other and added, 'They *were* there, honest. I didn't believe it any more than you do. I kept saying they weren't real.'

'You were saying that when we first saw you here,' said his father gently. Robin felt his face turning pink. He scowled down at the box full of Spitfire bits. It would be much nicer just to get on with making his aeroplane. The curtains round his bed had been drawn back now and Ward Sister, bustling past, saw the troubled expression on the faces of Robin's parents and came over to see what was going on.

'What happened next, old chap?' enquired his father.

'Well – there was this music,' said Robin. 'And Granny ran to the front door. And Callum was there and she went out to him. She went out there in the rain. Then the people brought them both in and Callum was pleased about the Dundee cake. It was very hot and crowded and my head started to hurt.'

'When we've had a bang on the head we think all sorts of funny things have happened, don't we?' said Sister briskly. 'Go a bit doo-lally for a while.'

Robin blushed again and his father said thoughtfully: 'There's more to this than meets the eye. Listen, Robin, did Granny give you any money?'

'A pound note,' said Robin promptly. 'Oh, and there was something funny about the change. It was different kind of money. Only I didn't get a chance to look at it properly.'

'It *was* different!' said his father triumphantly. 'They were old-fashioned coins, pre-decimal. Half-crowns and shillings and big pennies. You put it on the hall table, didn't you?'

'Yes,' said Robin.

'I counted it,' said his father. 'Seventeen shillings and threepence. Your cake cost two and ninepence, old money.'

'Lots of elderly people hoard bits and pieces of money,' said Sister reprovingly. 'We don't want to go believing any silly nonsense, do we?'

Robin stared down at the Spitfire box and wished everyone would go away. Something very strange had happened, but he had not invented it and he hated Sister's kind smile which said so clearly that she thought he had. Even his mother was looking half-hearted.

'Just a minute,' said his father steadily, and there was something in his voice which made Robin look up with new hope. 'I had a good look round Granny's sitting-room,' his father went on, 'after the police had gone and the poor old dear had been taken away to the Chapel of Rest. All the plates round the table had been used.' He held up a hand before Sister could say anything. 'Okay, it could have been the old girl shuffling from place to place having a nibble at each one. But the thing is, the shortbread was still on the cakestand, untouched.'

'Robin's mother nodded. 'I fetched it home yesterday,' she said. 'Seemed a shame to waste it.' But the others were watching Robin's father. 'The crumbs on the plates,' he said, 'were dark, curranty ones. They were the crumbs of Dundee cake.'

There was a silence. Sister glanced across the ward, suddenly interested in something else. 'Goodness,' she said, 'those flowers are a disgrace.' And she bustled off without looking back.

'Dundee cake,' whispered Robin's mother. 'Are you sure?'

'Absolutely certain,' said her husband. 'Didn't you notice? They're still there unless you've cleared them up.'

'I didn't somehow have the heart,' said Robin's mother. 'I thought I'd tackle it later.' Then she nodded slowly. 'Yes, you're quite right. They were cake crumbs. Why didn't it strike me?'

There was a long pause. Then Robin's mother gave a rather fluttery sigh. 'Well,' she said, 'as long as she's happy.'

Robin smiled at this echo of his own thoughts. 'I'm sure

she is,' he assured his mother. 'They both are.' He unscrewed the lid of his glue again. With all that tiresome business settled, he thought, he'd better get on with his Spitfire. They were sending him home tomorrow.

SEVEN

The Pin

Sitting in the bus, Julia's mother said, 'We are so lucky to have Emmie Small.' Julia did not reply. She hated Emmie Small. 'With this wretched war,' Mrs Purvis went on, 'the only way to achieve any style is to have a decent dressmaker.'

Julia stared through the slit in the shatter-proof webbing which had been pasted onto the windows as a defence against blast and which admitted a filtered, greenish light as if the bus was an aquarium. She did not want to achieve any style. The girls at school laughed at her because of the clothes she wore; cut-down afternoon dresses of her mother's in grey or mushroom, and lined skirts with a multitude of old-fashioned pleats. If only she had passed for the Grammar School, Julia thought as she stared out wistfully, she would have had to wear the uniform. The Grammar School girls looked wonderfully undistinguished in the shapeless navy blazers and skirts, with their ugly hats crammed on the back of their heads. At Gunthorpe Central only the first-year boys ever wore the black blazers with the green badge depicting three hammers; the blazers were never replaced once outgrown and the rest of the school wore what it liked. Or, in Julia's case, what it was allowed.

'That little suit of mine will do you nicely through the autumn,' said Mrs Purvis, 'once Emmie has altered it. There's a lot of warmth in crêpe-de-Chine, specially with a silk lining. And turquoise is so flattering. I always loved it as a child. Lilian preferred pink.' She gave a little sigh and folded her gloved hands over the amber clasp of her handbag. 'What these people do who had no wardrobe behind them at the outbreak of war I cannot imagine,' she said. Julia had a fleeting vision of her mother standing in her usual queenly pose before a huge mahogany wardrobe, but she did not laugh. The thought of the endless contents of that wardrobe was too depressing.

'Livermere Road!' sang out the conductor.

'Ah,' said Mrs Purvis. Despite the lurching of the bus she got up and made her way to the platform with dignity. Julia, clutching at the rails along the top of the seats for support, sometimes hated her mother as much as she hated the dressmaker.

'Now, you can run along to Emmie's by yourself, can't you,' said Julia's mother as the bus left them on the pavement. 'Wait for me there and I'll pick you up. I just want a few things.' There was no point in arguing.

The houses in Livermere Road formed a continuous terrace. Each house was approached by a tiled path and a flight of steps to a front door recessed under a brick arch. The garden gates had once been important-looking affairs with large stone balls surmounting piers of brick on either side of the entrance, but the gate and railings had been sawn off to make aeroplanes at the beginning of the war, and the privet bushes which most people had planted in their place looked raw and inadequate.

Emmie Small's house had a Judas tree in the front garden holding up crimson, woolly spikes of blossom. Julia looked up at the windows where the heavy curtains were never more than a few inches apart even on the brightest day. Emmie Small is a witch, she thought.

The edge of the curtain twitched, and Julia knew she had been seen. The door opened as she mounted the stone steps. Emmie Small's name did not suit her. She was a fat, flabby woman with thick wrists and a large, pale face. Her pale blue eyes bulged. She looked past Julia and asked, 'Where is your mother?'

'She's gone shopping,' said Julia.

Emmie Small closed the door behind Julia, shutting out the daylight with it. 'Come through,' she said.

Julia followed the bulky figure in its brown and yellow dress across the dim hall. She particularly hated that dress. It was a sort of mobile exhibition of dressmaking art, with an unneccessary number of hand-worked buttonholes and hand-covered buttons and, despite its many tucks and darts and gathers and its hand-made belt, it somehow failed to fit. It was aggressively odd, and it wore Emmie Small's thick body inside it like a picture Julia had seen once of a boa-constrictor eating a donkey. The grey hair pinned into a bun on top of Emmie's head seemed to be trying to escape the threat of the engulfing collar and Julia wondered if the woman's eyes bulged for the same reason.

In the back room with its barely-parted curtains Emmie said: 'If you'll just slip your things off.' She never smiled. A brownish light filtered through a tortoiseshell shade above the old-fashioned treadle sewing-machine, and the jacket of the crêpe-de-Chine suit was draped on the dressmaker's dummy which stood in the corner. White tacking threads ran round its sleeve edges and its hem. 'I've put two darts in the back,' said Emmie Small, offering the jacket as Julia reluctantly pulled off her jersey in the stuffy room, 'but you're such a match-stick, aren't you.'

The suit was dreadful. Julia stared at herself in the long mirror. She looked middle-aged although the jacket's long revers hung slackly over her Chilprufe vest and the skirt barely cleared the top of her socks. 'It's a bit long,' she said.

Emmie Small frowned at Julia's sandals and said, 'You want a nice high heel.' She knelt down with a little grunt to hitch the turquoise skirt up higher at Julia's waist, squinting critically at the effect. 'I wouldn't like to spoil the line,' she said. 'No, it's best as it is.' She moved, still kneeling, round to Julia's back, tweaking at the jacket, pinning and re-pinning. 'Most girls your age are getting a nice little shape,' she said.

Julia stared across the room at the dummy, senseless and

dignified with its turned mahogany spike sticking up where its head should be, and raged inwardly. The dummy was Emmie Small's ideal person, she thought, brainless and unprotesting, accepting her pins just as Julia was expected to accept her pricking little remarks. 'I just don't think I'll ever like this suit,' she said, and her voice shook.

Emmie Small was unmoved. 'Stand up properly,' she instructed through a mouthful of pins. And the dummy, with its long, sloping bust, seemed to smirk with its faceless face. Julia felt a wild desire to assault it, to demolish its smug dignity. It could complain to its mistress as much as it liked – afterwards.

'If you'll just slip the jacket off,' said Emmie Small. 'We'll see what your mother says about the skirt length. Mind the pins. Ouf–drat!' Letting go of the jacket as Julia began to wriggle out of it, she sucked a finger and Julia felt pleased. Well done, that pin, she thought.

There was a ring at the doorbell and Emmie said: 'That is probably your mother.' Still sucking her finger, she left the room. Julia inspected the crêpe-de-Chine jacket in search of the pin which had done the damage. To her pleasure, she found it. A minute smear of blood dulled its point. Julia removed the pin carefully and, holding it out like a dagger, she tip-toed across to the dummy. 'And it can prick you, too,' she said to it. 'Horrible thing.' She thrust the pin up to its head in the dummy's centre where the two halves of its calico body were joined with an almost invisible seam.

She turned away quickly as she heard the dressmaker coming back with her mother, and pretended to be looking at herself in the long mirror, smoothing the hideous skirt with her hands.

'She thinks it's too long,' said Emmie Small. Her pale, broad face was as impassive as ever. 'But with those pleats right up to the waistband, it's not easy to shorten. It would add quite a lot to the cost.'

'I do think it's wise to allow for growth,' said Mrs Purvis

smoothly. She gave Julia a cursory glance and added: 'No, that's fine.'

Julia took the skirt off and scrambled back into her jersey and the ink-stained pinafore dress which she had bought for ninepence at a school jumble sale for the Red Cross. Her mother sighed at the sight of it and Emmie Small said, 'Some of them take a long time to develop any taste.'

'One can only try,' said Julia's mother heroically.

Julia dawdled along the pavement when they had got off the bus on the way home. 'Oh, do come *along*,' her mother snapped. 'Take your hands out of your pockets and walk properly!'

Julia scowled. She did not want to do anything properly. She wished she could be a tramp, wearing any old clothes that came to hand and never having people nagging about style. It was the same at school – all those dried-up old teachers looking at you as if you were a nasty smell. The only one who was any good was the married one, Mrs Lee, who taught history. Her lesson about witches had been really interesting. She'd been saying how people were ready to believe any old rubbish just because they wanted someone to blame for all the nasty things that happened. So they accepted the idea that witches caused cattle sickness and swine fever, and they believed all that stuff about sticking pins in a doll that represented a person, so that the person would die.

Julia stopped in her tracks. Her mother turned and raised her eyebrows. '*Now* what's the matter?' she enquired.

'Sorry,' said Julia hastily. 'I just thought of something.'

'What?'

'Oh – just something silly.'

Julia had thought of how she had rammed the pin all the way home into the body of the dressmaker's dummy. She felt a secret, savage thrill. She could have killed Emmie Small. No more visits to the gloomy house, no more dreadful made-over garments. But then she reminded herself that nobody believed in that kind of rubbish any more. There were no witches. No dolls that represented anyone. It seemed a pity. She stared at the pavement as she walked beside her mother, and took short steps so that she would not have to tread on a join between the slabs, for that would be bad luck.

Julia's father was a quiet man. He came home from the office at twenty-past six every night and after high tea would sit reading a book until the daylight faded and it was time to start getting ready to go to the air raid shelter in the garden. There were frequent air raids that summer and Julia's mother had decided that it was less disturbing for the family to go to bed in the shelter than it was to migrate there from the house when gunfire woke them from sleep.

Julia lay in her bunk and stared at the concrete ceiling. The planks which had held the wet cement in place had left the stamp of their grain deeply printed in the grey surface and Julia knew the pattern of each plank intimately. From the bunk below her came the soft scratching sound of her mother filing her nails. Her father continued to read by the light of the Hurricane lamp which hung from a nail in the wall.

Julia hated the shelter. Despite the ventilation brick in the wall, condensation formed on the ceiling and dripped from the wood-patterned concrete so that the blankets were always damp, and the place smelt of wet clay. She hated almost everything, she thought dismally. Perhaps it had always been like this. People had lived uncomfortably, hating the difficulty of it all and wondering why it couldn't be different. A sunny day and a blossoming of wild flowers would make them feel that things could be easy and beautiful, so that when the well dried up and the grass browned in the fields and everything was hard again, they wanted somebody to blame. No wonder there had to be witches.

Julia remembered how she had looked up at Emmie

Small's house and thought that the dressmaker was a witch. Regretfully, she supposed that she had needed a witch; a scapegoat to blame for everything. Emmie Small was the obvious person to choose. Her fat, pale face and the scraped-up hair were so unattractive and the checked dress so hideous. But, Julia reflected, Emmie Small was not clever enough to be a witch. Witches were feared because of their ability to do strange things with herbs and plants, and because they owned mystic books and could understand how animals thought. Emmie Small did not even understand that the garments she made were ugly. I'd be a better witch myself, Julia thought with a flicker of pride. That's what I'll say next time they ask me what I want to do when I leave school. I'm going to be a witch.

The bunk shifted a little as Julia's mother replaced the nail file in her leather manicure case, and Julia heard the webbing creak as it always did when anyone turned over in the make-shift beds. Her mother was settling down to sleep. It was quiet in the dark garden outside. No raiding aeroplanes had come yet although the warning siren had sounded earlier, at dusk. Julia thought of the leaves on the cherry tree rustling a little in the cool night air – while the humans lay buried in a smelly hole in the ground. Hopeless tears suddenly burned in her eyes. Her father closed his book and turned out the Hurricane lamp. A smell of paraffin wafted up from it as Julia wept silently in the stuffy darkness.

When Julia got home from school the next day her mother said, 'We have had a blow.'

'Something to do with the war?' asked Julia. People were always sitting round the radio with grave faces.

'Oh, *no*,' said Mrs Purvis irritably. 'Something personal. Emmie Small is dead.'

Julia stared at her mother and felt her face flush with guilty delight while her skin crawled. The pin. She had killed Emmie Small by sticking that pin into her dummy with a mind full of hatred. I *am* a witch, thought Julia. I really am.

'You don't have to look so thunder-struck,' said her mother. 'She wasn't killed by a bomb or anything. She just had a heart attack – or so they think.'

One must always attack the heart, Julia thought wildly. She remembered how the pin had scrunched a little as she pushed it into the heart of the horsehair body. She wanted to laugh.

'It seems her brother came to visit her,' went on Mrs Purvis, 'and when he arrived the blackout curtains were still drawn and she didn't answer the door. He had to get the police to break in and they found her dead in bed.'

Julia felt faintly disappointed. It would have been much better if the dressmaker had been spreadeagled over the sewing machine, with the dummy fallen across her like a corpse itself. But at least she was dead.

'You'd better call in tomorrow and collect that suit,' said Mrs Purvis, glancing crossly at her unaccountably smiling daughter. 'You can pick it up on the way back from school.' She sighed. 'I suppose I shall have to try and finish it myself, and I *loathe* sewing. Such a *menial* occupation. Goodness only knows where we shall find another dressmaker.'

Julia got off the bus at Livermere Road that afternoon and approached Emmie Small's house without reluctance. A large black car stood outside it. Undertakers, she thought happily. Today, the curtain did not twitch as she walked up the path. She knocked on the door and waited. It was opened by a man with a large, pale face. He wore a black tie which looked odd with his droopy linen jacket and he stared at Julia without speaking.

'I came to collect a turquoise suit,' said Julia. She was suddenly embarrassed by her mission. 'I – I'm sorry,' she added. 'I mean – it's not finished. My mother said she would be in contact with you about the account.'

The man nodded, unsmiling. 'You had better come in,' he said. From the dim hall Julia caught a glimpse of the two undertakers through the open sitting-room door. They were sitting very upright on high-backed chairs, wearing black suits and each holding a top hat on his lap as if it was a cat. The man made a faint gesture towards them and said: 'I have things to attend to. If you could find the garment you want from my sister's workroom –' He indicated the door across the hall.

'Thank you,' said Julia. He had the same turn of phrase as Emmie, she thought. If you could just slip your things off. She went into the room and pulled the heavy curtains as far apart as they would go, letting the dusty sunshine stream in. The worn Turkey carpet looked shabby in the ruthless light and the dark green plush cloth on the table was faded to a yellowish brown. The crêpe-de-Chine suit hung among some other garments on a dress rail, the tacking stitches in its sleeves and hem unchanged. For a moment Julia was tempted to leave it where it was and tell her mother that it had disappeared; but she knew she would never get away with it. Her mother was a far more formidable opponent than Emmie Small.

Julia looped the jacket and skirt over her arm. Then she crossed the room to the dummy. In the middle of the centre seam, where the two halves of its sloping bust came inwards to a slight depression, the pin's head gleamed in the unaccustomed sunlight. Julia picked at it with her finger nail to free it from the tight calico, then pulled it out. She held it carefully between finger and thumb, and stared at it. Emmie Small's blood still dimmed its tip. Julia smiled. Then she turned back the hem of the dreadful maroon silk dress she had been wearing at school that day, and threaded the pin into it. She drew the curtains back to their usual shrouded position, and left the room.

That evening after high tea Mrs Purvis got out her little-used work basket and sat frowning over the turquoise jacket. 'I've absolutely nothing that matches,' she said, poking impatiently at the tangled mass of cottons and darning wool. 'Of course, you wouldn't think to bring the thread she was using, would you.'

'No,' said Julia baldly. A kind of courage was growing in her which was quite new. Her mother shot her a threatening glance then, with much difficulty and at arm's length, threaded a needle with some green cotton. 'I sometimes think,' she said tightly, 'you simply don't appreciate what's done for you. How many girls at your school have clothes of this quality?'

'Actually, they think my clothes are weird,' said Julia recklessly. I shall be a witch, she thought, and everyone will be afraid of me.

Mrs Purvis gave a contemptuous laugh. 'Girls like that have no idea,' she said. 'Their *parents* have no idea.' She stabbed short-sightedly at the jacket, holding her head on one side and squinting at it through narrowed eyes.

'Why don't you wear your glasses?' asked Julia.

'I *hate* wearing glasses,' snapped her mother. She glared at Julia with compressed lips then burst out, 'Why – why – why! Why did I get married and have you, that's what I should ask!' Julia's father glanced up from his book as if he was about to say something, then resumed his reading. 'I was a fool, of course,' his wife raged on in the beginning of a tirade familiar to Julia and her father. Her fingers shook as she put a couple of large stitches in the jacket, looked at the result and crushed the jacket in her lap. 'I was too generous – too ready to give my love with no hope of return. And where has it got me?' She swept a contemptuous arm round to indicate the room. 'Just look at it. A dull, poky little house in a dreary suburb. Lilian wasn't like me. *She* didn't fall in love, *she* didn't throw herself away. Everyone said she was cold and calculating, and maybe she was. She waited for a man who was worthy of her – and look at the result. A beautiful place in Dorset, servants, horses, parties, holidays, acres of parkland – and now Bernard is dead she's inherited the lot.'

She turned on Julia furiously. 'You know the best thing you can do?'

Julia looked enquiring. She had heard it all before. Her father gave a little cough and turned a page.

'Just pray that a bomb drops on this house, that's all,' Mrs Purvis shouted, 'when you're safely at school. With me good and dead, they'll probably send you to live with Auntie Lilian. God knows your father couldn't look after you. You'd like that, wouldn't you, living like the lady of the manor down in Dorset. It's what you want, isn't it, once you've got me out of the way. *Isn't it?*'

'Yes,' said Julia stonily. She was supposed to cry at this point, then her mother would hug her and assure her that it was all right. But it had happened too often.

'*Oh!*' Her mother buried her face in her hands. In the next instant she snatched the turquoise jacket from her lap and hurled it at Julia, then jumped to her feet and ran through the open French window into the garden.

Julia watched her. The drama made her coldly angry. Her mother was leaning against the cherry tree with her hands behind her and her head thrown back to gaze sightlessly at the fluttering leaves as she wept.

Julia's father cleared his throat. 'It's this war,' he said. 'Getting her down. She's very highly strung.'

Julia turned on him. 'So it's all *my* fault?' she asked.

'Well –' Her father looked uncomfortable. 'You could try not to upset her.'

'I've always tried,' shouted Julia, 'and where has it got me?' She clenched her fists. If she was not careful, she thought, she would sound exactly like her mother. But Dad was so infuriatingly meek. Her father shifted a little in his chair and returned to his book.

Mrs Purvis entered into a vitriolic silence which, Julia knew, would last for the best part of a week. She would speak brightly to the milkman and the postman but not to her family. It was a familiar pattern.

That night Julia took the pin with her to the shelter, secretly placing it in a gap between the bricks in the wall. Her mother was already in her bunk, aggressively silent and with the blankets pulled up over her shoulders to exclude the light of the Hurricane lamp.

In the darkness after her father had turned the lamp out, Julia lay awake for a long time. She thought about her Aunt Lilian who, with her white-haired husband, had come to visit them once. Far from being the cold, calculating person her sister had described, Lilian remained in Julia's memory as relaxed and smiling. It had been a lovely afternoon. Julia's father had laughed at the baggy slacks Lilian wore and she had teased him about his panama hat. He had talked more that day than Julia could remember him talking since.

Mrs Purvis began to snore. For a woman of her dignity she snored very loudly and the rattling vibrations of it made the bunk where Julia lay above her feel as if it was shaking. Julia hated the close, intimate sound so much that she began to sweat, lying rigidly in the dark with clenched fists. It was almost with relief that she heard the sound of distant gunfire. If the enemy aircraft were coming this way, the noise might wake her mother and stop her snoring. She thought again of her mother's oft-repeated accusation that Julia wanted her to die. What if a bomb really should fall on the house during the day? It would be wonderful to go and live with Aunt Lilian. She would see her father from time to time, of course, but it did not seem to matter very much about him, one way or the other. He so seldom said anything that he was almost like a piece of furniture – just a familiar object in the background.

The gunfire grew louder and the drone of engines vibrated through the night air. It was an ominous sound, but the snoring of Julia's mother was closer and more permanent. Aunt Lilian's house was deep in the Dorset countryside, safe from enemy aircraft. If she lived there, Julia thought, she would not have to sleep in an air raid shelter or wear anybody's cut-down clothes. She would have a room of her own, with satin-striped wallpaper and lacy curtains tied back with ribbon, and in the morning she would look out across sunlit parkland where ponies grazed, and there would be breakfast on the terrace. Her fingers crept across the brickwork, feeling their way to the crack where she had placed the pin.

If it did not work, she thought, there would be no harm done. If it did, she would live with Aunt Lilian. Nobody would suspect her. People didn't believe in witches these days. People were such fools. Julia took the pin firmly between finger and thumb, her third finger laid against its point so that she could guide exactly where it was going. She wriggled to the edge of her bunk and reached down in the darkness. The gunfire was getting louder. She felt the rough blanket which covered her mother's shoulder and moved her fingers, still gripping the pin, cautiously across it. The whine of a falling bomb began. Julia's fingers sought urgently for her mother's uncovered skin.

The explosion seemed to bring the walls of the shelter together like clapped hands. Julia's mother woke with a strangled snort, flinging out an arm which caught Julia's exploring hand and drove the pin into its guiding finger.

'By heck,' said Mr Purvis, who had also woken, 'that was close.' He struck a match and lit the paraffin lamp. Julia, huddled under her blanket and sucking the salty blood from her pricked finger, pretended to be asleep. Emmie Small had sucked her finger, she thought, clammy with fear. But then, she told herself, Emmie Small had not been a witch. She, Julia Purvis, was a witch, and she could not be harmed by her own spell.

Mr Purvis got up and put on his tin hat and dressing-gown. 'Just take a look round,' he said. After a while he came back and reported that the bomb had dropped on the back of Woolworth's. Nobody answered. Mrs Purvis had remembered her anger and Julia was still pretending to be asleep. He got into bed and turned the lamp out.

Julia was trying hard not to panic. The pin, she reasoned, had killed Emmie Small through being stuck in the dress-maker's dummy, not into the woman herself. And Julia Purvis, she thought with a flash of perception, was a kind of dummy to her mother. Was she not a mere doll to be dressed in what clothes her mother liked, a possession to be caressed or screamed at according to its owner's whim? Yes, Julia thought, that was probably the way it worked. If so, she would have done the trick by stabbing her own finger, no matter how accidentally. She smiled. Then she decided that it would be sensible to carry out her original plan – just to make quite sure. She would wait until her mother began to snore again. She lay in the dark and held the pin tightly, waiting. But, despite the throbbing of her pricked finger, drowsiness crept over her and, nursing the lovely thought of murder, she fell asleep.

Mrs Purvis did not attempt to wake Julia the next morning until her husband had gone to catch the eight-fourteen as usual. Then she came to the top of the wooden steps which led to the shelter and said with some satisfaction, 'You are going to be late.' There was no answer. 'Julia!' shouted her mother. It was against her principles to speak to the girl at all but – she sighed – to be a mother involved one in constant sacrifice. Mrs Purvis shouted again but there was silence from the shelter. Tight-lipped, she made her way down the steps and thrust aside the grey blanket which acted as a door curtain. It fell again behind her as she went into the stuffy, clay-smelling darkness. She began to shake Julia by the shoulder, then gave a gasp. 'Oh, no,' she said. 'No.' With sudden violence she wrenched at the blanket curtain, tearing the drawing pins out of their wooden batten.

The daylight confirmed her fear. Mrs Purvis burst into a flood of tears. 'Julia!' she wept. 'I can't bear it! I can't bear it!' She clasped her daughter's dead hands between her own and raised them passionately to her lips. She felt a sharp prick in the underside of her nose and involuntarily dabbed at it with the back of her hand. She looked at the line of blood left there and then found the pin clamped between Julia's stiff fingers. With a muffled exclamation she snatched it from her daughter's grasp and threw it on the shelter floor. It was the last straw that even in death the child should ruin her mother's expression of grief with some crude absurdity.

At twenty-past six Mr Purvis came home to find his wife lying face up under the cherry tree, one hand gracefully extended in the grass, the other laid across her breast. Her dead face wore a look of patient suffering which was slightly spoiled by a bluebottle which squatted on the underside of her nose. He shooed it off then called the police, who subsequently found Julia's body in the air raid shelter.

The neighbours took pity on the shocked man and looked after him for some days while autopsies were conducted and an inquest held which recorded a verdict of death from an unknown cause in both cases. When the funeral was over Mr Purvis thanked his neighbours politely and went back to his house. There, he washed the breakfast dishes which had remained untouched since the fateful morning nearly two weeks ago, and tidied the kitchen. He went to the shelter in the garden, folded the blankets neatly and retrieved the book he had been reading. He noticed a pin lying on the concrete floor and automatically picked it up and tucked it into the back of his jacket lapel, for he was a tidy man. He noticed that the blanket curtain had come away from its batten and replaced the drawing pins to hold it properly. He went back to the house and packed a bag with a few clean clothes and some favourite books, then sat down at the dining-room table and wrote cheques for all outstanding bills. The last one was from E. Small, Dressmaker. A heavier hand had totalled the crabbed figures and had added the words, 'Final

Account'. Mr Purvis wrote out the small cheque and attached it to the bill with the pin he had found in the shelter. For a dressmaker, he thought with something approaching a smile, it seemed fitting.

That night the house received a direct hit and was totally demolished. News of this reached Mr Purvis some days later in the form of a letter from his neighbours, brought out to the terrace by the maid at breakfast time. He read it, then passed the letter to Lilian. He shrugged in response to her enquiring glance. 'It was a poky little house,' he said, and tapped the top of his second egg.

EIGHT

The Glass Game

Karen stared round her room dispiritedly. Downstairs, her father played 'The Holly and The Ivy' on the piano. She supposed he was entertaining Mr Judd. It would take more than that, she thought, to make this place seem Christmassy. The sloping ceiling, the flower-papered walls and the gabled window which looked out onto the silent woods, somehow held a brooding sadness which would not be dispelled.

The house had seemed unhappy when they first came to it but they thought it was simply suffering from its long period of emptiness and neglect. 'An unloved house,' the estate agent had said sentimentally, and Karen's mother had clasped her hands in pity and said: 'Oh, Bill, we must have it.'

Four acres of woodland surrounded the huge house, the remains of a much larger shooting estate now sold to the neighbouring farmers. The gamekeeper's cottage stood by the gateway to the drive and was inhabited by the taciturn Mr Judd. Karen's father, being an architect, planned to divide the house into large self-contained flats whose tenants would enjoy the shared amenities of the wooded grounds and the long-overgrown tennis court, and Karen had at first agreed enthusiastically that it was a marvellous idea. But the sadness of the house persisted. At the turn of a stair or looking out from a high window over the tree tops, Karen found herself chilled by a wave of unhappiness which caused her to stand absolutely still where she was, her mind and body paralysed by a nameless grief. And one day she had found her mother sitting on the low window-sill on the first floor landing, with tears running down her face.

Now it was Christmas. Karen's father finished 'The Holly and The Ivy' and started on 'God Rest Ye, Merry Gentlemen'. Karen sat on her unmade bed, reflecting with grim humour that her room could not be more of a tip if merry gentlemen themselves had been carousing in it. Clothes lay about on the floor and a welter of holly-patterned wrapping paper was left from last night's duties with the Christmas presents. Karen, along with her father and mother, had assumed at first that a cheerful clutter would soon wake the house up from whatever nightmare it slept in, and turn it into an ordinary, warm, untidy home. But it hadn't happened.

Karen stood up reluctantly. She would have to go downstairs and help with Mr Judd. She almost laughed as she left the cluttered room. Mr Judd was the last straw. He was so silent and awful that he made the sadness of the house seem positively hysterical. As she started down the stairs she thought sombrely that they could not go on living like this. Something had to happen.

Bill Hadfield, striking the last chords of 'Deck The Hall', looked up from the piano with relief as his daughter came into the room. Mr Judd, having refused the comfort of armchair or sofa, sat on a high-backed wooden chair at a respectful distance from the fire, with a glass of whisky cradled in his large, bulky-knuckled hands. He looked stiff in his dark suit and waistcoat and occasionally ran a finger round his collar. His faded ginger hair curled in yellowish fronds round the back of his neck despite his evident efforts to plaster it down, and his face was as grooved and folded as the bark of a tree, the eyes narrowed as if perpetually squinting down the sights of a gun. Karen found him unbearably creepy. She had been appalled when her mother had said she was going to invite him to spend Christmas Day with them, but Ann had said crossly: 'What can I *do*, Karen? He's got no relatives to go to and I can't bear the thought of the old boy sitting in that cottage all on his own at Christmas. After all, he is our tenant. I feel responsible for him.'

Bill had pointed out that most landlords did not feel like that about their tenants – but Mr Judd had duly been invited, and had arrived on the doorstep with his tweed cap in one hand and a Christmas card in a rather grubby envelope in the other. Ann Hadfield had admitted to Karen in the kitchen that the man had few social graces. 'He just doesn't talk, does he?' she said. 'I suppose gamekeepers spend so much time on their own, they get out of the habit of talking.'

'He's not a gamekeeper now,' Karen had said. 'He hasn't gamekept for years. I think he's just plain horrid. He gives me the creeps.'

Her mother had looked distressed. 'Oh, dear,' she said. 'I did so hope we'd have a nice Christmas. In spite of everything.' Karen did not need to ask what she meant.

As her father got up from the piano, smiling valiantly, Karen seized a plate of mince pies from the sideboard and advanced upon Mr Judd who sat as incongruously as a piece of agricultural machinery against the pink velvet curtains. 'Do have one,' she said.

'No, thanks,' said Mr Judd.

Ann came in from the kitchen. 'Does anyone fancy some tea?' she enquired. 'Or is it too early yet? How about you, Mr Judd?'

'I'm all right, thanks,' said Mr Judd. Behind him, the winter sun was level with the tree tops. Frost had sparkled on the grass all day.

'Spot of sherry for you, Ann?' offered Bill. 'Mr Judd, top up the whisky?'

'I'm all right,' repeated Mr Judd.

Nobody wanted sherry. Bill put another log on the fire, dusted his hands and remarked: 'Well! There we are.'

They all sat down. There was a long silence. Rather desperately, Karen's mother cleared her throat and said,

'I'm sure we ought to get on Christian name terms – it seems so formal to keep calling you Mr Judd. I'm Ann and this is Bill. Karen you know, of course.'

Mr Judd nodded.

'So what's your first name?' persisted Ann.

'Ezekiel,' said Mr Judd.

Karen smothered a hysterical giggle. Her mother gave her a reproachful look. There was another long silence. Ann picked up a magazine and began to leaf through it, trying to look as if she found it interesting. Bill changed his mind and helped himself to another sherry. Mr Judd did nothing. Karen stared at him with covert hostility, hating the unrelaxed bulk of him. She hated his smell, too. Despite overtones of aftershave, there was a sharp, earthy reek about him which was quite foreign to the room. It would have been all right without Mr Judd, she thought. Despite the uneasiness of the house, she and her parents could have found some way to enjoy Christmas, if only in companionable silence. There was nothing companionable about any silence which included Mr Judd.

Karen decided that she must stop moaning to herself about it, or the afternoon was going to seem endless. They needed some activity. But what? The Hadfields had a weakness for old-fashioned parlour games like Consequences or Find a Rhyme, where you wrote the first line of a poem on a piece of paper then passed it to your neighbour who wrote the next one and so on – but she doubted the possibility of getting Mr Judd to write a poem. He probably wasn't much good at Scrabble, either.

It came to her in a flash. 'I know!' she exclaimed aloud, 'We could play the glass game!'

Ann closed her magazine at once. 'What a good idea!' she said, smiling at Karen. 'Why didn't I think of it? Just the thing for Christmas Day. Do you remember when we did it at Hallowe'en and the glass told Bill he was going to marry a mermaid?'

Karen laughed. 'In an old house like this,' she said with bravado, 'we should raise some wonderful spirits.'

'Count me out,' said Bill. 'Too spooky by half.'

'Oh, come *on*,' said his wife. 'It's only a bit of fun. I mean, I wasn't *jealous* of your mermaid.'

Bill smiled, shaking his head, and Ann turned to the man who sat stolidly on his wooden chair. 'Mr Judd –' she said, 'Ezekiel– you'll join us, won't you?'

Mr Judd was watching her suspiciously, stone-coloured eyes glinting from behind his narrowed lids. 'What is it?' he asked.

'You write each letter of the alphabet on a little bit of paper and arrange them all round a table,' Karen explained. 'In a big circle. And at one side you put the word, "Yes" and "No" at the other. Then you get a glass – just an ordinary glass – and put it upside down in the middle, and everyone sits round and puts a finger on it, just lightly. Then you ask it questions and it spells out the answers. It does actually move, you see. We've done it lots of times.'

'You shouldn't meddle,' said Mr Judd heavily. He took a gulp of whisky and wiped his mouth on the back of his hand. 'Leave well alone.'

Suddenly Ann showed a flash of annoyance. 'Look,' she said, 'we're trying hard to have a good Christmas, aren't we? At least, *some* of us are!' She glared at Bill, who responded at once. 'Sorry, love,' he said. 'Yes, of course we are. I'll go and get some paper.'

Mr Judd stood up, scowling in embarrassment at the reproof. 'No offence meant,' he said. 'I'd best be off.'

'No, of *course* you mustn't go, Ezekiel,' said Ann, repentant. 'Come over here and join us.' She was taking a bowl of nuts and a pile of magazines off the circular rosewood table which stood near the French windows. She drew the curtains against the fading daylight and said: 'We'll need another chair. Could you get one from the dining-room, Karen?'

'Okay,' said Karen. When she came back, Mr Judd had

returned to his original place, except that he had pushed his chair back against the wall so that he sat as far as possible from the rosewood table. Bill was writing a large letter on each of the slips of paper he had produced. 'Come on, Ezekiel,' he said, glancing up. 'Be a sport. Join in the fun.' The exhortation sounded entirely artificial.

Mr Judd's face settled into deeper furrows. 'I'd rather not, sir, if you don't mind.'

Bill shrugged. '*Chacun à son goût*,' he said, and began to distribute the letters at meticulously-spaced intervals round the table.

Karen got a heavy-bottomed tumbler out of the sideboard. She had learned from experience that stemmed glasses were apt to tip over in moments of excitement.

'Right,' said Ann when the three of them were sitting at the table. 'Off we go, then.' They each extended a hand to lay a finger lightly on the inverted glass. Mr Judd watched them, scowling.

'Is anyone there?' said Karen.

'Got to give it time to warm up,' said Bill. 'Like an old-fashioned wireless set.'

Ann leaned forward a little. 'Are you there?' she asked the glass earnestly. 'Is anyone there?'

The glass gave a small twitch and Karen felt the prickle of slightly fearful excitement which made the game so enjoyable. Hesitantly, the glass inched its way across the surface of the table towards the word 'Yes'. When its rim touched the edge of the paper on which the three letters were written it paused as if to gather energy then slid back to the centre of the table.

'Who are you?' asked Karen.

More strongly this time, the glass slid to the letter P, then to its neighbour O, skirted round the N, the 'No' and the M to touch twice on the L, then in a long, skidding rush, charged across the table to the Y.

'Polly!' said Karen.

'Yes! Yes! Yes!' agreed the glass in three excited dabs, then ran back to the centre of the table where it shifted restlessly from side to side as if anxious to be spelling out further messages.

Karen and her mother glanced at each other, smiling. There was something very engaging about this little spirit.

'Polly–' Ann began, and then stopped, suddenly aware that Mr Judd had got to his feet and was standing in what seemed an absurdly theatrical posture behind the standard lamp, a hand to his averted face as if to try and hide himself from view. 'Mr Judd,' said Ann, abandoning her attempt to use his Biblical forename. 'Are you all right?'

Mr Judd glared furtively from behind his hand. 'I best go,' he said.

Ann half made to get up and Karen said quickly: 'Don't take your finger off the glass, Mummy! We might lose the spirit!'

'What's dead is dead,' said Mr Judd, and added loudly, 'Just leave it, you hear me!'

Karen felt the glass shift uneasily under her finger as if flinching from the strident voice, and her father unexpectedly said: 'Look, Mr Judd, just sit down, will you? Or help yourself to another whisky and then sit down. I share your feeling that all this is a bit creepy, but there's no harm in it. It's only a game. We'll be with you in a minute, right?'

Karen and her mother exchanged impressed glances at this amazing outburst from the mild-mannered Bill, and Mr Judd subsided, muttering.

Karen bent to the glass again. 'Polly,' she said, 'who are you? Or who *were* you?'

The glass had begun to move in response to the first question, not waiting for its amendment. 'C-h-a-m-b-e-r-m-a-i-d,' it spelt.

'And where were you a chamber-maid?' asked Ann.

'H-e-r-e.'

'Here in this house?' Karen was fascinated.

'Yes.'

'Good Lord!' said Bill.

Ann said: 'Tell us more about yourself, Polly. Did you have a boy friend?'

'Yes.' And, unasked, the glass ran to and fro across the table so quickly that their fingers almost parted company with it. 'A-l-a-n,' it spelt.

'Did you marry Alan?' asked Bill kindly.

'No.' The glass paused, then slowly crept to the letters which spelt: 'D-e-a-d.'

'Oh, no,' said Karen – but the glass was moving again. 'C-r-y,' it spelt, then repeated the word. 'C-r-y.' It crept back to the centre of the table and there wove a small, side-to-side pattern like somebody rocking in grief.

'Oh, Mummy,' said Karen as she felt the hair on her head begin to prickle. 'It's the house. The sadness.'

Her mother met her gaze and nodded slowly.

'I knew we shouldn't have started this,' said Bill. But nobody suggested picking up the glass and abandoning the game. It was as if some wild creature had come to feed, and they held their breath for fear of breaking the trust it felt in them.

'Polly,' said Karen carefully, 'what happened to Alan?'

In that instant there were two simultaneous events. Mr Judd leapt from his chair and bolted across the room, but stopped dead in his tracks as there came a thunderous knocking at the French windows.

Everyone jumped and Ann gave a little scream. 'Keep your finger on the glass!' said Karen single-mindedly as her father, who sat nearest to the curtained French window, involuntarily turned to it. With his free hand, he twitched the curtain back, unlocked the door and pushed it open. 'Come in, whoever you are!' he called.

Karen held her breath; but it was a reassuringly normal young man who stepped into the room, curly-haired and healthy-looking, jacketless and with his sleeves rolled up over weather-tanned forearms despite the frosty evening. The glass began to gyrate impatiently, swinging in crazy circles until it spelt again and again: 'A-l-a-n, A-l-a-n, A-l-a-n!'

'Yes, I know,' Karen said to it in amusement. 'You want to tell us what happened to Alan. Just hang on a minute.'

'I came to wish you a happy Christmas,' said the young man calmly.

'How nice!' said Ann with her finger following the gyrating glass. She was flustered at being caught by an unexpected visitor while committed to playing this game. 'Look, Mr – er –'

'Carter,' said the young man.

'Mr Carter, we're delighted you've come to see us,' Ann went on. 'It's the first time anyone from the village has paid us a visit and it's lovely to see you. But we're playing this game at the moment, so you'll have to help yourself to a drink, if you don't mind. Over there on the sideboard.'

'It's nice you won't leave the game,' said Mr Carter. 'I like that.' Ignoring Ann's offer of a drink, he pulled up the chair which Karen had brought in for Mr Judd and sat down on it. 'Keep your fingers on the glass,' he said, nodding approval. Then he stared blue-eyed across the room to where Mr Judd stood in rigid terror. He gave a soft laugh. 'And I came to see Ezekiel,' he said.

'If you've got some business to discuss,' said Bill, looking from the young man to the old one, 'you could, er –' He obviously did not quite know what to suggest.

'Our business has waited a long time,' said the boy. 'But it will soon be settled now.' Karen, glancing across at Mr Judd, saw the man try to extend a quivering hand to the door knob. It seemed an impossible task. The veins on his forehead bulged and he let the hand drop, leaning back against the door as if in pain. Karen wondered if he was all right. The glass twitched restlessly under her finger.

'I'm sorry you haven't been too happy in this house,' said

the curly-haired boy, looking at each of them in turn with his blue eyes. 'It will be better now. You'll see. Go on with the game.'

'I hope you're right, Mr Carter,' said Ann gravely. Then she returned her attention to the glass. 'Polly,' she said. 'Tell us what happened to Alan.'

Sliding from letter to letter and returning momentarily to the centre of the table between each word, the glass steadily spelt out its story. Another man had loved Polly; an older, jealous man. He had threatened to kill her if she went out with anyone else.

The boy called Carter looked up to where Mr Judd still stood rigidly against the door. 'I think you should come over here, Ezekiel,' he said pleasantly. 'This'll interest you.'

The glass was off again on a new chapter of its history. Polly loved Alan, but Alan could not come to the house. Alan was a poacher and she met him secretly in the woods on moonlit nights. 'A-f-r-a-i-d o-f m-a-n,' it ended.

'Come along, Ezekiel,' the boy insisted with a hint of menace. 'Over here.'

As if hypnotised, the man moved stiffly to the table and stood staring down at the glass. Karen was too fascinated by the unfolding tale to take much notice of dreary Mr Judd.

'But what *happened*, Polly?' she asked. 'How did you die?'

'M-a-n k-i-l-l-e-d m-e.'

'The man you were afraid of?'

'Yes.'

'But why? Because he was jealous?'

'Yes.'

'Polly,' said Bill with morbid interest, '*how* did he kill you?'

'R-a-b-b-i-t s-n-a-r-e. W-i-r-e- r-o-u-n-d n-e-c-k.'

'Oh, God, how awful,' said Ann, revolted. 'I hope the police caught him.'

'No. C-a-u-g-h-t A-l-a-n.'

'Alan! Oh, no! But why?' Karen stared at her mother in anguish as she asked the question, and saw the same distress reflected in Ann's face.

'I'll tell you why,' said Mr Carter, and the glass was at once still, as if listening to this unexpected interruption.

'Alan was a poacher,' the boy went on. 'And the man who killed Polly was a gamekeeper. And when this man had left her lying in the wood he went and told the police he had found a dead girl with a rabbit wire round her neck, and said a poacher must have done it. Very upset, he sounded. Alan was on his way through the wood to meet Polly, not knowing what had happened, when the police caught him. And there were rabbit snares in his pocket.'

The glass was moving again, creeping from letter to letter. The boy was silent as they watched it. 'H-a-n-g-e-d.' it spelt.

Horror turned Karen's joints to water. 'Hanged Alan?' she asked faintly.

'Yes,' said the glass. And the boy nodded slowly.

'But that's awful!' exclaimed Ann.

Bill, in an attempt to lighten the atmosphere, looked up at Mr Judd who was standing over the table with the crazy stillness of a lightning-struck oak tree. 'May as well sit down, Ezekiel,' he said. 'Take the weight off your feet. You're making the place look untidy.'

Mr Judd did not move.

'Sit down, Ezekiel,' said Mr Carter pleasantly, 'when the gentleman tells you.'

Mr Judd perched uneasily on the arm of the sofa. His shoulders were hunched and his clenched fists pressed together. Karen had been thinking furiously. 'If you know all about what happened,' she said to the curly-haired boy who sat facing her, 'then you must know who the man was who did it. The name of the gamekeeper.'

The glass jiggled excitedly under her fingers and the boy gave a short laugh. 'I know, all right,' he said. 'And so does Polly. But we're the only two.'

The glass shot to the edge of the table, almost sweeping off the piece of paper with the letter E written on it. Then it careered across to the Z, back to the E, and dived so fast for the K that it slipped out from the three fingers resting on it. For a moment it stopped dead but the instant their contact was resumed it was away again. Karen and her parents had already realised the name it was spelling, and stared at each other in consternation as it darted to the letter I.

Mr Judd, suddenly galvanised, jumped to his feet, his face suffused with a dull purple colour. 'That ain't right!' he shouted. 'You can't prove I did it!' He lunged at the table, reaching out a hand as if to snatch up the glass.

'It was *you*!' screamed Karen, recoiling as the man's arm brushed past her face. Mr Judd's fingers touched the glass and there was a sharp crack, like the sound of a pistol shot. The heavy-bottomed tumbler shattered, sending fragments of glass flying across the table, and Mr Judd buckled at the knees. He collapsed face down across the table, and the pieces of paper with the letters written on them flew up like confetti. His knobbly, rigid fingers clawed for a grip on the polished rosewood surface, dragging across it with a dull, scraping sound as he fell slowly to the carpet among the fluttering scraps of paper and the shards of glass.

The young man moved politely out of the way as Karen's mother and father rushed round the table to the fallen man. Karen herself had her hands pressed to her face as if to smother the silent scream which filled her mind. The young man looked at her. 'I'm sorry,' he said gently. 'But things will be better now. We will look after you, Polly and me.' And he turned, parted the curtains and walked out of the French windows.

'Hey!' Bill shouted after him. 'You can't just go like that! You're a witness!' He scrambled up from where he had crouched beside Mr Judd and ran to the open French windows. 'I'll have to call the police!' he shouted after the boy. 'I think this man's dead – and what about the business you had with him?'

There was no reply.

'We don't even know what his first name is,' fretted Ann, who was kneeling on the carpet beside the dark heap of Mr Judd's body. 'Just Mr Carter. It's going to sound so silly.'

But Karen, in a tingling shiver, knew with utter certainty what the boy's first name would be. 'Alan,' she whispered. And distantly, from across the frosty lawn where no footprint disturbed the silver grass, the young voice echoed Karen's whisper as if amused that something so obvious should need to be stated. 'Alan!' it said. Then, as they stared at each other in the quiet room, it added more faintly, 'And my business – is finished.'

Karen crossed to where her father stood at the open French window. A full moon had risen and they could see clearly. The garden lay still and empty.

While Bill was dialling 999 Karen said, 'I think I'll go up to my room for a bit.'

Ann looked at her daughter's white face with concern. 'Yes, of course, darling,' she said. 'Shall I come with you? Are you all right?'

'I'm all right,' said Karen. 'I just don't want to stay in the same room as – him.' She did not even want to look at the inert heap which lay so incongruously by the rosewood table.

'I'll bring you up some tea in a minute,' said her mother. She paused. 'It's – it's all very funny, isn't it?'

'Very funny,' said Karen. As she left the room she heard her father saying firmly that he was not under any circumstances going to play that blasted glass game again.

She climbed the stairs slowly, opened the door of her room and switched on the light. Then she gasped. The bed was made, its corner turned down in a professional way, ready for the night. The magazines were neatly stacked on the shelf, the clothes returned to their hangers, the wrapping-paper folded up, the dressing-table tidy and dust-free. Karen's mind raced. Apart from a few seconds in the kitchen, her mother had been in the sitting-room all afternoon. There had been no time when she could have come up and tidied the room. Yet it looked as if an expert chamber-maid had been in and taken care of everything.

A chamber-maid. For a moment Karen felt panic, a wild surge of alarm which made her scalp crawl. But it was at once replaced by a comforting warmth which was utterly new to the house. 'Polly and I will take care of you,' the boy had said. Karen opened the window and leaned out in the frosty air. It was almost dark now. A police car was coming up the drive with its blue light flashing, but it seemed insignificant under the huge yellow disc of the moon which hung above the dark mass of the woods. A perfect night for a lovers' meeting, thought Karen. The air was cold. She pulled the window shut, drew the curtains and sat down on the tidy bed with a small, happy sigh. 'Thank you, Polly,' she said. But Polly was out in the woods with her true love, and did not reply.

There was a loud knock at the front door, followed by the sound of men's voices in the hall.

'Karen, dear!' Ann called up the stairs. 'Could you come down for a minute? The police are here.'

'Coming!' Karen called back. With a last look round the warm, tidy room, she switched out the light and started down the stairs. The coming interview was going to be very strange. But she was perfectly sure of one thing. Her father had been right; none of them would ever play the glass game again.

You can see more from Mammoth
on the following pages . . .

Also by ALISON PRINCE

Haunted Children

They were all quite ordinary children – Emma who was waiting for the train, Edward who had a birthday party, Christine who went to the dentist – but that was before it happened . . .

Sometimes slowly, sometimes fast: but for all the children in this spine-tingling collection of stories, familiar, everyday things turn into strange, horrible or terrifying events.

MARGARET MAHY

The Haunting

'When, suddenly, on an ordinary Wednesday, it seemed to Barney that the world tilted and ran downhill in all directions, he knew he was about to be haunted again.'

Tabitha can't help noticing the change in Barney – how quiet he's become, his pale expression and those dazed eyes which seem to be seeing things from another world. But, as Tabitha determines to solve the mystery she finds herself in very deep waters.

'Strong and terrifying . . . The novel winds up like a spring. A psychological thriller.'

TIMES LITERARY SUPPLEMENT

Compiled by LANCE SALWAY

The Magnet Book of Spine Chillers

At first they seem harmless enough – a school outing to a museum, a cage full of budgerigars, a teddy bear – but eerie things can and do happen to the most ordinary people.

Six favourite children's writers have joined forces to show you just how strange – and frightening – some people and places can be!

Compiled by LANCE SALWAY

Shivers in the Dark

There was something very odd about Mr Dickins, the new teacher. It wasn't just his bright red hair and sharp, pointed teeth. Perhaps it was the way he taught arithmetic by setting his fingernails alight . . .

Jane was overjoyed when she heard about Joanna coming to stay. 'I bet we'll get on like a house on fire,' she said. How could she have known how prophetic her words were to be . . . ?

Compiled by LANCE SALWAY

Shivers in the Dark

There was something very odd about Mr Dickins, the new teacher. It wasn't just his bright red hair and sharp, pointed teeth. Perhaps it was the way he taught arithmetic by setting his fingernails alight . . .

Jane was overjoyed when she heard about Joanna coming to stay. 'I bet we'll get on like a house on fire,' she said. How could she have known how prophetic her words were to be . . . ?

ERIC MORECAMBE

The Vampire's Revenge

In the small village of Katchem-by-the-Throat, in the tiny country of Gotcha, a fierce storm was raging. The jagged lightning struck one of the statues in the park – and out crawled someone very stiff and dusty indeed! An evil smile flickered painfully over his bloodless lips. 'Wotcha, Gotcha, I'm here to getcha!'

Eric Morecambe's rumbustious sequel to **The Reluctant Vampire**

A Selected List of Fiction from Mammoth

While every effort is made to keep prices low, it is sometimes necessary to increase prices at short notice. Mammoth Books reserve the right to show new retail prices on covers which may differ from those previously advertised in the text or elsewhere.

The prices shown below were correct at the time of going to press.

☐	416 24580 3	**The Hostage**	Anne Holm	£1.50
☐	416 96630 6	**A Box of Nothing**	Peter Dickinson	£1.75
☐	7497 0186 2	**The Granny Project**	Anne Fine	£2.25
☐	416 52260 2	**Sarah's Nest**	Harry Gilbert	£1.50
☐	416 51110 4	**Zed**	Rosemary Harris	£1.75
☐	416 54720 6	**Changing Times**	Tim Kennemore	£1.75
☐	7497 0344 X	**The Haunting**	Margaret Mahy	£2.25
☐	7497 0130 7	**Friend or Foe**	Michael Morpurgo	£2.25
☐	416 29600 9	**War Horse**	Michael Morpurgo	£1.75
☐	7497 0051 3	**My Friend Flicka**	Mary O'Hara	£2.99
☐	7497 0228 1	**The Vandal**	Ann Schlee	£1.75
☐	416 51880 X	**Journey of a Thousand Miles**	Ian Strachan	£1.75
☐	416 95510 X	**Ned Only**	Barbara Willard	£1.75
☐	416 62280 1	**Archer's Goon**	Diana Wynne Jones	£1.75
☐	416 22940 9	**The Homeward Bounders**	Diana Wynne Jones	£1.50

All these books are available at your bookshop or newsagent, or can be ordered direct from the publisher. Just tick the titles you want and fill in the form below.

Mandarin Paperbacks, Cash Sales Department, PO Box 11, Falmouth, Cornwall TR10 9EN.

Please send cheque or postal order, no currency, for purchase price quoted and allow the following for postage and packing:

UK	55p for the first book, 22p for the second book and 14p for each additional book ordered to a maximum charge of £1.75.
BFPO and Eire	55p for the first book, 22p for the second book and 14p for each of the next seven books, thereafter 8p per book.
Overseas Customers	£1.00 for the first book plus 25p per copy for each additional book.

NAME (Block Letters) ....

ADDRESS ....

....